NO RETURN TICKET

NO RETURN TICKET

Clyde Packer interviews nine famous Australian expatriates including Robert Hughes, Gordon Chater, Germaine Greer, Maxwell Newton, Zoe Caldwell and Sumner Locke Elliott

ANGUS & ROBERTSON PUBLISHERS

ANGUS & ROBERTSON PUBLISHERS
Unit 4, Eden Park, 31 Waterloo Road,
North Ryde, NSW, Australia 2113
and
16 Golden Square, London W1R 4BN, United Kingdom

This book is copyright. Apart from any fair dealing for the purposes of private study, research, criticism or review, as permitted under the Copyright Act, no part may be reproduced by any process without written permission. Inquiries should be addressed to the publishers.

First published in Australia by Angus & Robertson Publishers in 1984

Copyright © Robert Clyde Packer 1984

National Library of Australia
Cataloguing-in-publication data.

Packer, Robert Clyde, 1935–
   No return ticket.
   ISBN 0 207 15028 1.

   1. Australians — United States — Addresses, essays, lectures.   2. Public opinion — Australia — Addresses, essays, lectures.   3. United States — Social life and customs — 1980-   — Addresses, essays, lectures.   4. United States — Foreign opinion — Addresses, essays, lectures.   I. Title.

973.927

Typeset in 11pt Palatino by Graphicraft Typesetters Ltd
Printed in Hong Kong

CONTENTS

Author's note	1
Robert Hughes	5
Gordon Chater	29
Graham Fraser	44
Dame Judith Anderson	57
James Wolfensohn	71
Germaine Greer	85
Maxwell Newton	100
Zoe Caldwell	130
Sumner Locke Elliott	142

AUTHOR'S NOTE

This book is about Australians who live in America. Notwithstanding the impression given in the Australian press that the universe rotates around Australia, most people outside the major urban centres in America would have difficulty (despite Brian Brown, Mel Gibson and Helen Morse) picking out Australia in an atlas. Many are still pleasantly surprised to discover that Australians speak English. Yet Australians are to be found everywhere in America.

The book deals only with Australians who live in America and ignores the many interesting Australians who live in England and other places, for English Australians are a different type of animal and require a different type of book. Too many Australians who live out their days in England treat their nationality as a sort of social disease, which if assiduously treated can eventually be cured but if left untreated invariably becomes terminal — a view which has been shared by some Australians in Australia.

Readers may wonder why I chose *No Return Ticket* as the title for this book. It seemed to deal neatly with the various means of changing countries. A one-way ticket usually means a permanent arrival in a new country. Some people leave Australia on a one-way ticket; theirs are deliberate, permanent departures. Others leave with a round-trip ticket and just do not return. Sooner or later they cash the ticket in. This cashing of the ticket is often the cutting of the last firm link with home. It implies a commitment to a new life outside Australia.

Such a commitment does not, however, necessarily sever all ties with Australia, particularly today. A so-called "expatriate" myself, I often wonder whether satellite communications and jumbo jets have tempered the traditional perception of expatriates as being people who have turned their back on their country. The feeling of separation that moving to a new country used to involve has been almost eliminated by the variety of modern communications now available.

It would now be possible for Robert Hughes to fly from New York to Sydney in the time it would have taken Ireland's famous literary expatriate James Joyce to travel by train and ferry from Trieste to Dublin.

The international telephone, the cost of which seems to fall as its quality and ease of use rises, is a unique pipeline for family members separated by an ocean actually to hear each other's voices a few times a year. But if expats buy package trips home to Australia regularly and ring up Mum once a month, are they still expats? Not according to my dictionary.

I might have used "expatriate" in the main title but, like the physical distance between Australia and America, it is not what it used to be. The Anglo-Celtic writers followed by the Americans of the overblown bullfighter *American In Paris* period turned "expatriate" into a boring literary cliché. Any reality associated with the expression has long vanished. "Expatriate" English writers now huddle in their villas in Switzerland or Nice to avoid taxation rather than from any sense of alienation from their native land, jetting home for the twelve weeks in each year they can spend in London without attracting English tax.

Readers should note that Dr Germaine Greer, one of the first people I interviewed for the book, was living at the time of the interview for half of each year in America as is described in the interview with her. Shortly afterwards she terminated her arrangement with her American University and returned to live in London full-time. Now that her new book *Sex And Destiny* has been published she will certainly be offered several new posts in the US. Americans find her an engaging and provocative lecturer. I decided to keep her interview in the book for many reasons. I like her and I like the interview. The only important thing that has changed since the interview is her place of residence. The interview is not about teaching at an American university. It is about growing up and getting out from under.

This book could not have been written without the cooperation of the nine people whose stories it contains. Their generosity in time and spirit made this project a most interesting one for me. For that reason there is no private author's dedication. It is for them all.

A few people I talked to did not get into the book. This reflects solely on my ability to do something with the material I obtained. I can but apologise and once more thank them for their time.

The Angus and Robertson research staff in both Sydney and London were most helpful. The research was used for the purpose of preparing interviews and not validating them. What is written here is what used to be called *reportage*. I make no claims of veracity other than to state that what appears is an honest summary of what I have been told. The opinions are mine. I hope there are not too many of them.

Richard Walsh was anxious to publish this book, for which I am grateful. Also I was fortunate to have as my editor Norman Rowe, who has struggled to bring some sort of order to my tangled syntax.

My main difficulty in writing it in America has been getting my interview tapes transcribed. Multiple Australian accents on a tape baffled several American transcription services. Finally Maureen Lance, a Londoner, stepped into the breach with brisk efficiency.

I apologise to visiting Australians in Santa Barbara who have been forced to read chapters. Their corrections and suggestions have, however, proved invaluable.

I would also like to acknowledge the support and assistance I have, as always, received from my wife Kate.

Robert Clyde Packer
Santa Barbara, 1984

ROBERT HUGHES

I remember Robert Hughes as a young man in Sydney. He was almost too good looking and his masculine beauty was well matched by his virtuosity. He became, in rapid succession — not in any coherent order that I recall — a painter, a cartoonist, a poet, a critic and, from time to time, even a student of architecture at Sydney University.

Hughes is the youngest of three brothers born into a leading Sydney Catholic family. His grandfather had been a Lord Mayor of Sydney and his father a papal Knight. His elder brother, Tom, became a sort of father figure, after Mr Hughes Sr died when Hughes was twelve. Tom is T. E. F. Hughes QC, one of the leaders of the Australian bar, and a former Liberal MP and federal Attorney-General. Middle brother, Geoffrey, is a Sydney solicitor and a prominent Catholic layman busy in many religious and political activities. Hughes's mother was born an Anglican but converted to Rome in 1920.

Since the beginning of the 1970s, Robert Hughes has been possibly the most influential art critic in the English language. In saying this I am not making an unqualified judgement about art criticism. I am relying on the continuous publication of Hughes's work by *Time* and on the efficiency and dispatch with which the publishers of that magazine arrange for its almost universal availability within hours of publication, throughout the free world.

Hughes's television series, "The Shock of the New", an ambitious and highly successful undertaking produced for the BBC in the mid-1970s, broke new ground in making the principles of modernism and avant-garde art visually comprehensible to a mass television audience. Since 1974, he has been working intermittently on *Chains*, a book about Australian convicts.

With my wife Kate, I lunched with Robert Hughes at his Soho loft in New York one Saturday. His wife Victoria was in hospital. His household that day consisted of a parrot, an Australian sheepdog of surprising intelligence, and a friend of the Hugheses from Sydney, the actress Kate Fitzpatrick. The food, cooked by Hughes, was superb. He was fascinated by my new tape-recorder, holding it in his hand and talking directly into it. From time to time we went back and edited the grossest indiscretions. This is what remains of that conversation:

Robert Hughes, Sydney, 1980 (News Ltd)

PACKER: "You have said Alan Moorehead got you out of Australia."

HUGHES: "Moorehead encouraged me to leave Australia. He'd read some of the art criticism I'd been writing for the *Mirror*. This would have been 1961. He was in Australia for an Adelaide Festival, playing 'The Grand Returning Writer' — a familiar role. He rang out of the blue (we had no mutual acquaintances) and said: 'Look, I've read what you've been writing. I think it's good. Could I come and see you?' I said: 'Who are you?' He said: 'I'm Alan Moorehead.' Whereupon I made loud noises of obeisance and nearly fell through the floor with surprise. He came round, and we spent the morning getting drunk. I deluged him with quantities of unpublished stuff, which he waded through. He said: 'What you should do is leave Australia and go to Europe because you're not going to be able to find a publishing situation here which you can really develop. There aren't the papers; there aren't the magazines.' I'd been to Europe once before, having fallen in love with this ballet dancer and scuttled over to lay my mitts on her, in 1959. But, since I spent most of that time doing the 'Sorrows of Young Werther' because she dumped me in favour of some banker, I didn't really do very much when I was there."

PACKER: "You had an art exhibition to raise some money for your fare I seem to remember."

HUGHES: "I had a couple of shows. I used to sell paintings in order to subsidise myself as a writer. People used to buy my paintings with great alacrity, whereas I had some difficulty selling my writing. I couldn't possibly have made a living off art criticism in Australia."

PACKER: "I can remember having lunch with you one day. The late lamented Rudi Komon arrived in the middle of lunch and said, 'I need five more bushfires by eleven o'clock tomorrow morning'."

HUGHES: "I don't think it was bushfires, I think it was bulls or maybe it was snow. Yes, it may have been snow landscapes in Kosciusko. Dear! How I used to churn them out, and of course every one of them was deeply felt and seriously intended. Yes, I had a streak just before I went away. People were buying! Particularly the little gems. You know, twenty inches by ten. Goodness, how they used to lap them up in the Eastern Suburbs. They're now, of course, totally unsaleable. I'm a small refutation of the rule that the value of art goes up and stays ahead of inflation. Mine have gone down from the moment that they were painted."

PACKER: "But they got you to Europe?"

HUGHES: "I had about $2000 and set off. Alan said, 'Go to

London. I'll set you up with my publisher, Jamey Hamilton, I'll set you up with my agent, Lawrence Pollinger. You must try and crack it as a writer in London. If you fail you can always come down to Port' Ercole and stay with me for a bit.' He was careful to emphasise the 'for a bit'. I went via Las Vegas where I lost almost all of my modest stash. I met this floozie in Los Angeles and took her to dinner and after that I said, 'And where would you like to go now, my dear?' She said, 'I'd like to go to Vegas.' I thought it was a suburb of Los Angeles (which in a sense I suppose it is). Anyway there we were on this plane to Las Vegas. It has a slot-machine in the loo! Amazing object! In Las Vegas, I lost the girl and almost all my money, and crept on to London one wing low. I stayed in London for about six months and really bottomed out there. I rang up Alan and said, 'Listen, can I come down?' and down I went to Port' Ercole and I stayed with him and Lucy for about a month. I remained in Port' Ercole itself for two years."

PACKER: "What were you doing there?"

HUGHES: "I was trying to write a book on Dada and Surrealism, and this without a single reference library for this purpose within reach of Port' Ercole, I might add. Most of the time I spent getting drunk. It was a very peculiar period."

PACKER: "What were you living on?"

HUGHES: "I had a few paintings back in Australia; by Fairweather and people like that. I flogged them to live on. I would wander off and go over all the hill towns, and see every provincial museum in central Italy — long tours looking at art. This turned out to be of tremendous benefit to me. When you're from Australia, you think you know nothing; and everybody you're meeting, even the guy who runs the fish in the Naples market, you naively suppose to be a repository of the Renaissance. In point of fact (it takes you years to discover this) the Italians and the French are almost seraphically indifferent to their national heritage, and most of them don't give a fuck about painting, sculpture and architecture. They're much less conscious of it on the whole than the average bloke in Broken Hill."

PACKER: "So this was really your training for what became your life's work?"

HUGHES: "Exactly. It enabled me to overcome my inferiority complex about not being an heir of Europe. It enabled me, when I ran into an Englishman who was talking about Piero della Francesca, to think, 'Yes I know that Piero della Francesca too. I have seen it. I have my opinions about it.' It was the belated equivalent of a proper university art-history course, except it was conducted in rather a gutsy manner, with a great deal more passion; and wasn't done from slides. So one's inferiority complex was more or less conquered. I didn't discover that I had conquered it until I got back up to England in '66."

PACKER: "So you had about two and a half years?"

HUGHES: "In Italy, yes. It wasn't *La Vie de Grande Luxe*. The only people I really knew were Alan and Lucy. But then, you see, everybody has to have a mentor. Possibly if I'd gone into the law, my brother Tom might have played that role, but I didn't."

PACKER: "Germaine Greer says you are still a Catholic."

HUGHES: "If I am a Catholic, I'm a very peculiar one. Most of my fundamental intellectual constructs were given to me before the age of sixteen by the Jesuits. But, if being a Catholic means believing in a personal god, a literal heaven, a real hell and the primacy of the Catholic Church, which it does, I'm not Catholic. I'm allergic to Catholicism though I respect it. Our family lost too much to the Catholic Church for me to feel any obligation to it. When I go back to Sydney and see the prime real estate which was given to the nuns by my imprudent ancestors and then sold off by the Church to a bunch of developers, I still feel indignant. I'm not bitterly anti-clerical, but I'll tell you, I've seen too much of the Church. When Germaine says I'm fundamentally a Catholic, I know what she means because there's a sort of Jesuitical cast of mind that never leaves you. You're capable of entertaining two sides of the question. It's a method of argument which is not ultimately based on Loyola but upon classical structures transmitted through seventeenth-century education. But I'm extremely glad I had that education.

"Anyway, I went back to London in '66, because I was getting a bit sick of mucking around by the side of the Mediterranean. I'd learnt quite a lot, but I wasn't going anywhere. I'd had a spasm of intense anxiety, at one stage, about being a writer at all. It was because I wasn't in contact with any writers of my own age. I had my mentor in Alan. He was invaluable, indispensable. He gave you a model of professional conduct. He'd get up at seven o'clock in the morning, go into his study and stay in there until twelve. Almost always he'd come out with 1000 words. Now I couldn't do that, because all that *enfant terrible* stuff in Australia had conditioned me to think that I could rely upon inspiration, whatever that meant. What I would do in order to court the muse would be to drink all day and all night, and

---

The young artist, Sydney, early 1960s (News Ltd)

get up in the morning with a bit of a hangover and try to write something and of course I'd fail, and then, lo and behold, it was time for lunch. Later on, I found out what Alan was trying to tell me."

PACKER: "Was it different to what you thought he was trying to tell you?"

HUGHES: "It was a bit. It was about perspiration, keeping at it. No book is ever written unless you keep at it. And for that you have to have some reasonably secure area. It doesn't have to be sacrosanct or anything. It just has to be a secure area where you won't be disturbed for a certain number of hours each day. That's why Elaine's is an odd place. It's like the Sargasso Sea. There are all these ships with their keels entangled in the long weeds and they all sit there until four o'clock in the morning moaning about why they can't get their books finished."

PACKER: "I can't understand the mystique. I'm not a New Yorker but it seems to me an uncomfortable bar."

HUGHES: "It's uncomfortable, the food is bad, it's expensive and it's full of international white trash. I haven't been there for years. I don't agree with its pecking order. New Yorkers are sadists by day and masochists by night. They like to be discriminated against by headwaiters. American democracy breeds virulent forms of snobbism. Hence Yanks imagine Australians are egalitarian, which we're not. I prefer Australian to American snobbery, because it's more often based upon deeds rather than money."

PACKER: "Two or three times in stuff I've read about you, you have referred to your London period rather gloomily."

HUGHES: "Well, I had some good times. It wasn't all bad in swinging London by any means, but I had a very uppy-downy time, partly because of my marriage."

PACKER: "When did you marry?"

HUGHES: "In '67, in London. She was an Australian, a woman of many extraordinary qualities but also a flying test-bed for every fad that existed in the '60s. I don't have any animus against her, but I don't want to talk about marriage. In any case, we were divorced in 1981."

PACKER: "But you had a child?"

HUGHES: "A child, Danton, who was born in '67. He lives with her in Brooklyn, although he spends quite a lot of time with me over here now."

PACKER: "Does that chew you up a bit?"

HUGHES: "Oh, yes, but such was the agreement, and he, being now fifteen, will probably come to spend more time with me as time goes on. Anyway, the '60s were a pretty fraught time for everybody in London. I am by nature somewhat conservative, but I was trying not to be when I was in London. I went off several deep ends. I'm glad that I wasn't permanently harmed. Acid did a lot of people in, but the naivety was worse. Take this pill, smoke this herb, and the world will change. There was something babyish about the quality of hope in London then, particularly in those around Oz. It was a difficult time for anybody to develop as a writer because of the prestige that formlessness and spontaneity enjoyed."

PACKER: "Nihilistic?"

HUGHES: "I found it nihilistic. Everybody used to talk about peace and love, even the murderers like Malcolm X and his hitman, a truly frightening black thug."

PACKER: "Rip-offs?"

HUGHES: "Lightly disguised as revolutionaries. You do not know discomfort until you have sheltered the Living Theatre."

PACKER: "And the Australians?"

HUGHES: "Perhaps not quite as bad as some. There were some that I loved, and still do — mainly Richard Neville. I didn't like the climate of the '60s. I didn't like those promises of immediate salvation through instant renewal. I didn't like all that 'give it to me now, give it to me now' stuff. I went along with it in order, I suppose, to save my marriage, and placate my friends. It was all just like the Royal Sydney Golf Club. But fundamentally, like most instinctive Tories, I don't believe that mankind is all that salvageable. I don't think that you can legislate people into virtue, and I don't think that people suddenly turn from carnivores into herbivores by just smoking pot. I remember discussing this with Albert Speer once. He described the rich menu of dope that the Führer was shoving into himself by the end of the war, and he said, 'Well, you know, some people, if zey are of a peaceable nature, when they use marijuana they go and lie down in the flowerbed and smell with the bees. Other people, if they are not of a peaceable nature, they get stoned and they think of better ways to kill Jews.' Since this comes from the source, I imagine that there must be some truth in it."

PACKER: "I want to put this in some sequence, this London experience. When I knew you in Sydney, I wouldn't have described you as being a Tory, but you were a man of fairly traditional views."

HUGHES: "Yes."

PACKER: "And you are again now. London was a sort of aberration?"

HUGHES: "I was, to use the cliché, exploring. The reason why I was attracted to looking at works of art in the first place (specifically Surrealism because Surrealism is the young man's art movement *par excellence*) is that I wanted an alternative to my Jesuit upbringing. The Surrealists argued, like Blake: 'Better to strangle an infant in its cradle than nurse unacted desires.' I thought, therefore, that Surrealism, and particularly Surrealist art (since my French was not good enough to read the poetry), promised some way out of the Catholic *impasse* I found myself in. That is why I started looking at works of art in the first place. They seemed to promise freedom. They still do seem to me to offer some kind of freedom, but not in the same way. If works of art don't offer you freedom — some sense of enlarged possibilities, a greater range of psychic choice — then there's not much point in looking at them. Italy, in a way, was three years with the unfound father. It was also three solid years of consulting, over and over again, the masterpieces of the past, studying the foundations, finding what one always returns to until one dies."

PACKER: "Did you learn Italian then?"

HUGHES: "Yes, I did. So I was able to read Dante in the original. I was able to connect myself to all this material. I did it in a rather haphazard way, but I did it. Anyway, I was anxious to get to grips with the Italian past. Not so much classical antiquity as the Renaissance. There is a time in your life when you are almost exotically in love with a new subject — you're young, the mind takes impressions like wax and holds them like marble. Or so I felt in Italy. Then in London, I had a basically illiterate love of the future — the cult of spontaneity and denigration of the sense of history that went with the '60s."

PACKER: "That's what you mean when you say you were low in London?"

HUGHES: "I was low in London because I felt culturally out of sync. Also, I did recognise that there was actually some point to some of the so-called underground. So, I didn't feel in sync with the people who took rigidly conservative stances against it either."

PACKER: "I wonder if 'The Shock of the New' could have been quite so authoritative, if you hadn't have had that period in London?"

HUGHES: "It was essential. But probably most of everything that happens to you is essential to your development. Were I to go back to London, were I given a time machine, I would probably live my life differently. I doubt I would have married the same woman, for a start. But these questions are meaningless. That's the way I did live my life. If, for instance, I'd gone the academic route and become a student at the Courtauld and Warburgh Institutes and committed myself to a life of art scholarship, I would never have been able to do 'The Shock of the New' because I would not have been able to handle the material journalistically. I'm very interested in the kind of information you can get across to mass audiences without damaging the subject. It used to be assumed that there was this mass audience out there which had no claims on intellectuals' attention. This was the view of Dwight MacDonald and Clem Greenberg — essentially the *Partisan Review* set in the '50s. Now, it's certainly true that on a medium like television you can't say everything about a work of art and it's also true that you can't disclose everything about art in a magazine like *Time*, or the *New York Times*. On the other hand, there's a great deal that you can say, and this can be done well or badly.

"At the moment, there is an audience for this material because of the circumstances of postwar education. You have for the first time a large, reasonably visually literate audience, in America at any rate, much larger than any such audience has been in France or anywhere else. I think the series did, in terms of popular consciousness, write some kind of *finis* to the idea of modernism as a continuously ongoing avant-garde phenomenon. This heretical proposition first came to be discussed in the mid-'70s, and certainly at the time that I began the series, it still seemed a very novel idea. By the time that we'd finished the series, it was three years later, and it was less novel. I think what the series did was run in the idea of modernism as a closed historical period."

PACKER: "You would maintain, then, that you are a journalist, not a critic?"

HUGHES: "Both. There is a wonderful phrase in French; people say that they practise *la haute vulgarisation*, which doesn't mean vulgarisation, it means intelligent general discussion which doesn't damage the work. This is what I attempt to do. I had to learn it elsewhere. I left Australia because there were things you just can't learn in Australia. Think how little there was to see in Australia. This is the situation that Mollison is up against now. That National Gallery should have started twenty-five years ago."

PACKER: "I notice you're critical of it?"

HUGHES: "I dislike the building, but the collection's essential. If you cast your mind back to what there was to see in Australian museums in 1963, there was no way that one could have educated oneself in the history of art from that. I wanted to have some reason for going on as an art critic. I'd been thrown into being an art critic entirely by accident. I was a cartoonist on the old *Observer*. Here were Michael Baume, Peter Coleman and I sitting around, all drunk, after lunch. Donald Horne, who was then the editor of that journal, came in and said, 'I've just fired the art critic. You must know something about art.' I was the only one not underneath the table, I was still sitting more or less erect, and so that's how I got it. Oh God, when I think of it! There's no possible way that you could start a career as an art critic in such a fashion today. People know more now. If you tried, you'd make a total ass of yourself in public. And the readership, being more sophisticated, would write to say, 'Get rid of this idiot'. The editor would too, although perhaps not quite so quickly in Australia as they would here in America. America has an unemployable proletariat created by the art-education system. Every year, 35,000 people graduate from American art schools with tickets saying they're painters, sculptors, potters. They have serious professional intentions — 35,000 people a year! The total population of Florence in the last quarter of the fifteenth century was 70,000 people and that included everybody, from Leonardo to the dustman. So every two years we secrete that many artists, art historians and potential critics here. The problem is not a lack of professional expertise. However, in this country the graduates write so very badly. Lucky for me."

PACKER: "You said earlier that everything that happens is accidental."

HUGHES: "Well, I didn't get up one morning and say: 'I'm going to go to Europe and then I'm going to get to America and then become the art critic of *Time*.' It never turns out according to the guidelines, in my experience. Eugene Istomin, as far as I know, wanted to be a concert pianist from the age of seven onwards, so I suppose you might say that he had a plotted career; he never became a lumberjack, anyway. It was never so simple with me because I didn't have a manual skill, a virtuoso skill of that kind. The people in the performing arts tend to emerge early as virtuoso."

PACKER: "But your training in Australia was actually quite good. You had the early schooling with the Jesuits which taught you to think. Then you had the architectural stuff at Sydney which you didn't finish, which must be handy for what you do now."

HUGHES: "Oh yes, absolutely. For instance, I can render a drawing of the Parthenon in 140 washes of Chinese ink in the full *beaux arts* manner which they stopped teaching everywhere in 1930, except Australia. Watch out Michael Graves."

PACKER: "Then there was your cartooning and your early criticism. Is Australia really a place where you make mistakes and survive them?"

HUGHES: "It's like the Woomera Range. You remember the

Jindavik, our national defence drone. We were all like early little Jindaviks; we'd rise off our launching pad amid much farting and flame, and then we'd crash twenty yards down-range, and we'd pick ourselves up and run round and get off again. The thing is you only have one chance in a place like America. Well that's an exaggeration, many people have more, but America tends to give you one chance and it's a huge big chance and if you grab the ball and run with it, it may change your life. In Australia, you get lots of chances, but they're all little chances. Nobody in Australia is going to pay me the kind of money for writing a weekly art column the way *Time* does. It isn't feasible within the given structure of Australian newspapers and magazines."

PACKER: "And obviously, *Time* is very good to you. I've never managed to find you at the office, so obviously they let you work at home. They don't care where you go as long as you turn it in."

HUGHES: "Exactly; they don't mind where I go and they pay the fares. But I always have turned it in."

PACKER: "And yet, Bob, you remain aggressively Australian."

HUGHES: "What choice do I have? It's not a pose. I remain an Australian citizen, not out of sentimentality, but simply because it would be absurd or opportunistic to change."

PACKER: "How did the convict book germinate?"

HUGHES: "When Alan Moorehead was writing that book of his, *The Fatal Impact*, about the arrival of the white man in the South Pacific, he showed it to me in manuscript so that I could vet it for possible errors about art. I remember reading it with admiration and I said to him: 'I wish I could find some subject that didn't have to do with art. Something connected with my deepest preoccupations.' He said: 'Give it time, you will.' He was right. In 1975, I did a series for the ABC on Australian painting. We were in Port Arthur, which I'd never been to before. It's the Paestum of Australia. This great creepy ruin. And what is it, our Paestum? It's a gaol. And as we were going over it, it occurred to me that there wasn't an available book which gave the whole story of what the convict system was like. There's an excellent administrative history by A. G. L. Shaw called *Convicts and the Colonies*, but it gives you very little sense of what it was like being a convict. It's history from above, not from below, although it's a standard text and a very good one. I thought, 'Heavens above, there must be scope for a book here!' That was in 1974. I then saw a New York publisher about it. At the time there was no interest in Australia in New York. But they took it in the end.

"Now, almost ten years later, the subject is hot. There is a lot

more interest in Australia in America than there ever was. This has to do with films. They have this picture of us as being the Poles of the South Pacific. You remember that great fandango about the Polish cinema in the late '50s and early '60s. Now, it's our turn. Twice a month, I go and lecture in remote campuses in Idaho or Indiana and after the lecture comes question time. The students ask, 'What about this great renaissance of Australian films?' I explain to them that we colonials, who for years have been culturally colonised by Hollywood trash, just like Jack Lang said, have now at last through sheer self-awareness and nationalistic effervescence succeeded in making our own rubbish. I try and point out to them that there are Australian films and Australian films. And they only see the very best of them. They don't see *Alvin Purple* or *The Women of Cell Block H* — well, some see that one. It's got a devoted lesbian following. But mostly they see the cream of the crop."

PACKER: "I was talking to an Australian writer recently who said the trouble with setting a novel or a film in Australia is that if you're writing a saga like McCullough, yes, that's all right, and if you're writing something quaint or weird, that's fine too, but she feels the huge US market is not yet prepared to accept Australians in a novel as ordinary people."

HUGHES: "Yes, why is this?"

PACKER: "Perhaps they don't think Australians are interesting?"

HUGHES: "Americans don't have a coherent picture of Australia. It's just cultural unfamiliarity. They want to think of Australia as being exotic, a distant pioneer country, pre-Freudian, pre-political — that's their fantasy, but it's very diffuse. You try to explain to them the realities of Australian economic life, and the realities of Australian population distribution, and they don't want to hear about it. If you tell them that most people live in cities with the same population density as LA, they don't want to know. They think it's all Bryan Brown, and the Qantas koala."

PACKER: "That's why 'A Town Like Alice' was so successful."

HUGHES: "God, it was as boring as 'Brideshead', without even the house."

PACKER: "I would have thought that as a member of a fine old Catholic family, you would have been rolling in the aisles when you watched 'Brideshead'."

Publicising *Heaven and Hell in Western Art*, Sydney, early 1970s (News Ltd)

HUGHES: "Naturally. I'm as much a snobbish ex-Catholic as anybody else. It's a poor novel, the work of a spiritual groupie. It's not Waugh being rude about other people's snobbery, which would have made it a great novel. It's Waugh manifesting his own spiritual parvenuism with a beatific vision of God as the product of the English class system."

PACKER: "Talking about God and classes, how do you fit into the *Time* corporate arrangement."

HUGHES: "I'm their tame cockatoo. I'm the sort of interesting white bird with the large voice and erectile crest that gives them a good squawk every week. I don't help run the magazine. As the subaltern said when asked about his role in the cavalry: 'My job is to lend tone to the brawl'."

PACKER: "I saw a lovely reference to you in a press cutting recently. Apparently some pommy critic said, reviewing 'The Shock of the New', 'How long are the airwaves going to be polluted by the antipodean honkings of this broken-nosed Australian thug?'"

HUGHES: "It was the *Evening Standard* critic."

PACKER: "And your response?"

HUGHES: "I sent him a cable saying: 'My nose is not broken but if you make one more reference to it, yours will be. Yours sincerely.' That was the last time that I got any condescension from the poms about my accent, which as you can see becomes broader with every cup of wine that I lower."

PACKER: "Nobody ever criticised Dylan Thomas for speaking with a Welsh accent."

HUGHES: "No, but Australians are fair game. This is one of the reasons why I'm writing this book. It's not to have revenge upon the English, although one theme of this book is that the early history of Australia is nothing other than the history of how, in that remote continent, the British invented the gulag. I don't mean extermination camps, but the gulag. The idea of the gulag as it now exists in Russia is essentially an English invention."

PACKER: "I suppose the concept of convict labour in an alien land is in some respects theoretically more oppressive than slavery in America. The owners did not have to look after the merchandise."

HUGHES: "Sometimes worse than slavery. Slaves represented property; convicts did not. You could wear the man out and go and get a new one from the government."

PACKER: "There was no economic incentive to provide decent conditions."

HUGHES: "They treated them very, very badly. I found a great deal of first-hand material on this. Memoirs of convicts and letters which some Australian historians told me didn't exist. Some Australians like to use the same quotations over and over again: it saves the trip to the library. When the poms started to condescend to Australians, their view was, 'Well, they're our convicts. They are *ipso facto* inferior beings.' It never occurred to them that it takes at least two people to make a convict: it takes one to commit a crime and another to find him guilty of it and ship him out. The idea that transportation was of their making (and therefore it wasn't up to them to condescend) simply never occurred to them. I know I'm talking about it as if I'm radically sensitive about it. I'm not; but I didn't expect to see this prejudice as late as I did. It still survived in 1959 when I was first in London. It's gone now."

PACKER: "But here you are, a successful man ..."

HUGHES: "With English friends, I have to say."

PACKER: "Yes, here you are in New York, the English-speaking capital of the world — what might be called the cultural capital of the free world anyway ..."

HUGHES: "Up to a point. Insofar as there is a single cultural capital, I suppose that's what it is."

PACKER: "... being published by one of the most influential magazines in the world ..."

HUGHES: "It sounds good, doesn't it!"

PACKER: "Living in a lovely loft with a ..."

HUGHES: "A new wife, a parrot and a dog."

PACKER: "... and a kid that's not too far away. Yet you feel this need to ...?"

HUGHES: "Go back to Australia?"

PACKER: "Yes."

HUGHES: "Of course. Look, Bernard Berenson used to say we only have a certain number of pennies to rattle in our cup. We are born empty and we accumulate experience; we accumulate within the first twenty years of our life (whether we know it or not) the basic subjects that are going to serve us as writers for the rest of our lives. Now, of course, it's certainly true that in many cases some later traumatic and extraordinary subject matter will sweep in upon a writer. That on the whole hasn't happened to me. I've never stumbled into the middle of a catastrophe, plague or civil war. Most of the writing that I've done has been about places other than Australia, art other than Australian art. But at the same time, you find that your early experiences create, shall we say, a leaning towards certain kinds of subjects. I don't know how to put it in a way that doesn't sound pompous. You have to make allowances, OK? Expatriation is very largely about Oedipal revolt, it is about the feeling that if you're not going to kill your father, at least you're going to kill him symbolically by getting away from him. You find a new father. You and I are members, probably, of the last generation that thought of Australia as being deeply insufficient. Today, a young Australian who wants to go to England or America or to the Near North (which our generation called the Far East) would be likely to do so without any particular feeling that they *had* to leave. But think of the way some people used to write about this question in our day; that it was either Australia or elsewhere, and he who left was, in some sense, betraying his country. Sid Nolan once gave one of the great answers to this sort of thing. At the peak of his success, a reporter got him at the airport in Sydney and asked him: 'Do you ever really think about Australia when you're in London?' And Sid answered: 'Oh, yes. Every night.' What you were supposed to do was stay behind and participate in that great cyclical adventure called 'The coming of age of Australian culture'. That was the great trick that Australian culture used to do. Every ten years or so it came of age; you remember that?"

PACKER: "Indeed."

HUGHES: "Today that feeling of division between one's homeland and the rest of the world is probably not as extreme for twenty-five-year-olds. But in my day it was. There was the feeling that you were holding your nose and jumping off the end of a springboard."

PACKER: "The same thing probably happened here."

HUGHES: "Absolutely, Americans who left to go to Paris. Paris was the place in 1925; London was the place when I was a kid."

PACKER: "And yet Australians are still not always generous with their expatriates."

HUGHES: "Australians have been very generous to me. I've been lucky so far. I've had my share of bad reviews and God knows I deserve them because I've given a few, but on the whole Australians have been very nice to me. I think they are easier on expatriates now because they see that it's one world. The last time I was back, my wife, who's an American, loved Australia."

PACKER: "Is your wife a New Yorker?"

HUGHES: "She's a Californian. And she sees in Australia what California was before it fell. Of course, this fall from grace happened in the mythical days before she was born. Victoria would love to go back. We did the full Brideshead trip, as it were. I took her around to see the various stained-glass windows at St Canice's featuring dead Hugheses in khaki, and she was of course deeply interested in this. You don't have it in California. I took her out to my brother Tom's station, to Malcolm Turnbull's place, and so on. She ended up getting completely gaga about it. As a matter of fact, so did I. There really is a quality to Australian discourse, the way people approach one another and relate to one another as families in Australia, which is infinitely desirable after living in America. I just like getting back there. It is, after all, the only family that I've got: people like Malcolm Turnbull, and my niece Lucy, Tony Larkins and the rest. I know them and by God they know me. Here, Vicky and I are on our own, except for friends. So that, and the landscape and the general beauty of the place, and the wine and the food and all the rest of it eventually made me feel very, very nostalgic when I got back to New York, and the feeling is still with me. Yet when you think, 'OK, so tomorrow, I go back to Australia', what are you going to do? I like it here in New York. What I want to do is work out some arrangement whereby I can live in perpetual winter. I would like to be able to go back to Australia for two or three months of the year and work there.

"I don't think that I'd want to own a place in Australia because I'd never be able to maintain it. I own a house in Italy, it's a small house and it has, I think, only half a roof. I haven't spent a night there in four years because to get the wife together and drag her over there for the weekend would cost something like $2000! What the hell. I can go up to my place at Shelter Island and spend a weekend there quite affably and get some fishing and shooting too. The same problem exists with Australia. You fly from here to Australia, it's what, $6000 per person? You couldn't do it regularly. So I would rather go back for a month or two per year. But every time I go back there I get land fever. I think, 'Yes, yes, I must buy something'. Some people actually succumb to it. Sidney Nolan, for instance, and Arthur Boyd have been buying up one historic house after another which they then proceed to endow to the nation as monuments unto themselves.

"You know, on one occasion in '72 I was in Bali. I was sitting on the beach and theoretically everything should have been fine. Things were going well between me and the first wife for a change. The food was lovely, the sunshine delicious, the climate, and the landscape and everything all one could desire. All I could think of when I got up in the morning was, 'Where can I get a copy of today's *New York Times*?' There's merit to the biblical story of the expulsion from Paradise and the angel with the flaming sword who was placed at the entrance. Once you pass a certain stage of journalistic innocence, and when you're working for *Time* or *Newsweek* or the *New York Times* or something like that, then you're past that stage of innocence; you can't go back; you become an info junky. You also like the access it gives you. I can ring up a museum and they'll open it on the day it's closed and I can go in and have a look on my own. If I want a photograph, they messenger the photo to me within two hours. That sort of thing is nice to have. It isn't because of me, of course, it's because of *Time*. Obviously, I'd love to write about things other than art in the future."

PACKER: "How did you feel about the '20/20' flop?" [An American Broadcasting Corporation current affairs show, similar to CBS's "60 Minutes". Hughes was replaced as compere after the first programme.]

HUGHES: "It was one of those strange moments. They had decided they were going to produce the world's worst television programme. The only thing that could be said in favour of me and my co-host was that at least we knew how to write our own lines. This was the one thing we weren't allowed to do. It was like being Miss World for a day. You were pulled into this peculiar universe where enormous sums of money are flung around. It was the classic imbecile Hollywood experience. All these characters in polyester, double-knit, sky-blue leisure suits disgorging staggering amounts of money on you, and for what? For literally doing nothing. For being less than an actor. For standing in front of a camera and uttering some lines which were not even yours."

PACKER: "What was the great criticism of your performance? That they couldn't understand your accent? Or that you talked too fast?"

HUGHES: "They didn't understand my accent and I talked too fast. None of these criticisms was made of 'The Shock of the New'. It was a different audience. A different audience and different lines."

PACKER: "Yes, thank heavens."

HUGHES: "I'm glad they junked me after one programme, because it was so badly done. I'm not trying to transfer the blame; it genuinely was inept."

PACKER: "We haven't done the sequence from the UK to the US of A."

HUGHES: "In 1969, I was still living in England. I was free-lancing, mainly for the *Observer* and the *Sunday Times* and doing a bit of stuff for the BBC. My television career started when I got back from Port' Ercole in '66. Lorna Pegram (who ended up producing 'The Shock of the New') was looking for somebody to do a spot on

Australian art for a programme, there being an exhibition of Australian art in London at the time; and they didn't have anybody in London who knew, or particularly cared, about Australian art who could look convincing on television. Somebody introduced me to Lorna and I did this spot, and it seemed to work. Then I started doing little pieces for BBC 2. Every week on BBC 2, there'd be a cultural news round-up programme. If there was a show of Miró, let's say, at the Tate, then you'd do a piece on that. Somebody else would do something on a current novel, or a play — whatever had happened in the cultural world that week."

PACKER: "How often did you do written art criticism?"

HUGHES: "Generally, when John Russell went away, I'd fill in for him on the *Sunday Times*. Then, I was commissioned by George Weidenfeld to do this book on heaven and hell in Western art. Weidenfeld tended to commission unsuitable people to write books on subjects which require definitive treatment, and which end up as coffee-table books. George will invite, for example, Arianna Stassinopoulos to write a biography of Picasso. No, no, please don't laugh, she's doing one. There are these terrible *mésalliances* that he's always proposing. Most of them fail. Anyway George would slide up to you at some dinner and say: 'My dear, I am boiling and bursting with ideas for you.' He looked at me and saw that I was probably a Catholic and so he invited me to write a book on heaven and hell in Western art. I thought: 'How absolutely wonderful: what a terrific idea.' He offered me more money than I'd ever seen for a book before in my life. I think it was about £2000 (at least £1500 of which I actually received). So I went ahead and wrote this thing and it became a *flop d'estime*. It was well reviewed and sold two copies. However, a copy found its way to Time-Life who were in the process of looking for an art critic. They picked me on the basis of this book."

PACKER: "So you were brought to New York from London?"

HUGHES: "Along with two other contenders: John Russell (currently art critic for the *New York Times*) who was then writing for the *Times* in London, and Pierre Schneider who was the art critic for *L'Express* in Paris and fluently bilingual. At that stage, I had just been left, not quite definitively, by my first wife, who had gone off to Algeria in pursuit of Eldridge Cleaver. So there she was in Algeria, pursuing the Living Theatre and the spectre of Black Revolution, and there I was, left high and dry, or high and wet, in London and very short of money. There is a firm there called Nathan and Nathan. They're private bailiffs. The world divides into those who know what Nathan and Nathan means and those who don't. In my ears, the

words Nathan and Nathan sound like a bell. A Pavlovian reflex is set off engendering flight. Under English law, bailiffs cannot force an entrance but if somebody happens to go in they can follow hard on their heels. I was very circumspect about who I opened the door to. My neighbours knew this. Nathan and Nathan were more or less on twenty-four-hour watch waiting to distrain my furniture and possessions. Early one morning, my telephone having long ago been cut off for non-payment, there was a scratching at the window. Outside was this Rumanian painter, Leonard Hessing, who had crawled along the ledge between our windows. I opened the window and Hessing said, 'There's a call for you from New York'. So I clambered out through the window and in through Hessing's window and there was this strange American voice going on about how they (not identifying who *they* were) wanted me to come over. He wanted to know if I wanted to work for *them*. I was slightly deranged, and thought it may be the CIA. My brother Tom was the Australian Attorney-General at the time. This fellow said, 'We want you to come over and try out'. I got extremely cunning and said something like, 'Well, I would prefer that you paid my fare'. And then he said, 'Oh yes of course, expenses too. How much would you need?' I said hopefully, 'A thousand dollars'. And the fellow, sounding rather disappointed that I hadn't asked for more, agreed. At which point my heart lofted like a bird.

So over I flew to America. All my English friends cautioned me against taking the job. They all said, as if one voice, 'You will be edited, you'll be turned into *Time* style'. The curious thing is that I've never had so little editorial interference from a magazine in my whole life. They don't rewrite me, they don't do any of that kind of thing. Which leads me to suppose that either, like the gentleman in Molière who discovered that he'd been speaking prose all his life, I had been writing *Time* style all my life, or else they are not the demonic rewriters that one had been led to suppose they were. When I got there I made it a condition of the employment that I should have a by-line. Up to that time, no *Time* writers had had a by-line."

PACKER: "You were the first?"

HUGHES: "Yes, I was the first *Time* writer to receive a by-line. They were considering introducing it anyway. Criticism is an individual act, it is after all the expression of opinions which are the result of refraction of a work of art through the character of the writer. There is, properly speaking, no such thing as nameless criticism. I refused

---

Presenter of the ABC's "Landscape with Figures", Sydney, 1975 (ABC)

to write for the *Times Literary Supplement* on those grounds."

PACKER: "Does it embarrass you to discuss the details of your arrangements with *Time*?"

HUGHES: "I make about $80,000 a year from *Time* plus expenses and stock options. I'm extremely lucky in that the Managing Editor doesn't have any very strong feelings or convictions about the visual arts. I hope that on reading this chapter he will not then suddenly decide to develop such convictions, because that would then make both our lives hell. In the old days, Henry Grunwald, who brought me into the magazine in the first place, was the Managing Editor. Henry was supposed to let the critics have their head. But he is the son of a Viennese opera composer and has a long background in music. This made life difficult for the music critic because Henry had pronounced views of his own, not to mention extensive friendships throughout the musical world. So the music critic was edited closely. Not me; and I have always striven to discourage the people on the thirty-fourth floor from becoming art collectors."

PACKER: "Have you ever felt that you'd like to do some architectural criticism for *Time*?"

HUGHES: "Yes, that's a thorn in my side. I have written about architecture on occasions. Architecture in America, at the moment, is a very hot subject. There is no possible way I would be able to do both the art column and architecture column at the same time. I used to write the odd architecture story. It was not a satisfactory arrangement because I couldn't pay as much attention to one as to the other. The architecture scene in the United States is tremendously active now. It's very complex, riven with all sorts of ideological splits and discords."

PACKER: "How often do you go to the office?"

HUGHES: "I would say three days a week. I spend three days a week on art criticism working for *Time*. I try and do three to four days a week out in the country working on *Chains*, my convict book — 'Kangeroots'."

Visiting Sydney, 1981 (ACP)

GORDON CHATER

When he came to Australia, Gordon Chater was already twenty-four, but it was here that his career really started, and where he was to live for more than thirty years. It was his performance in an Australian play that finally took him to New York, and there he is regarded as an Australian actor. Now in his early sixties, he lives and works in the American theatre but flies back to Sydney when he is offered a part in a show he likes. I decided to include Chater in this book because his distinguished career in Australian theatre and television is a significant part of the history of these media in this country.

Gordon Chater was, he says, an afterthought. He was born in England in 1922, when his mother was forty-two years old. She was his father's second wife, and Chater her first child. At his birth, apparently still-born, he was chucked into a kidney bowl by the attending doctor — "Poor little bugger, he'll never play rugger". Fortunately, the nurse picked him up and administered an avant-garde, 1922 form of mouth-to-mouth resuscitation.

Chater's father was a chartered accountant, one of ten children who all grew up to establish impeccable middle-class credentials in the army, law, stockbroking and accountancy. His father had it all mapped out for Chater. He would follow him to Haileybury, one of the top English public schools, then move on to Sandhurst for a safe and proper career in the British Army.

However, when Chater was five, he was accidentally taken to the theatre. His mother went to a matinée and took Chater because she couldn't find a sitter. Afterwards they had tea with Granny, who asked Chater what he wanted to be when he grew up. To everybody's horror, he announced that he was going to be an actor.

As a young man, Mr Chater Sr had lost his savings when he was persuaded (by an Australian, oddly enough) to invest in a new play starring Lily Langtry. The play flopped. Chater discovered later the play his father had invested in was George Bernard Shaw's *Arms and the Man*. Mr Chater henceforth held sternly dubious views on the theatre, especially as a way to earn a living. Chater's mother was convinced that the theatre was rife with amorality, having been jilted, before meeting Mr Chater, by a theatre-owner.

At Haileybury, Chater donned drag at the age of thirteen when he played Queen Gertrude in *Hamlet* and got his first review, in the

---

Gordon Chater, Sydney, 1984 (News Ltd)

school magazine: "Gordon Chater as Queen Gertrude was the only one who knew what to do with her hands." That was also about the last time he played Shakespeare, although after three years living in New York, he has been told that his American accent is now good enough for him to attempt the Bard!

Chater went up to Cambridge in 1939 at the age of seventeen to study medicine. While at Cambridge, he appeared in a couple of productions of the Cambridge Mummers, directed by G. H. Rylands. He also performed with another undergraduate company in *Hands Across the Sea* by Noel Coward. He went so well that he was encouraged by friends to seriously think of giving up medicine for the theatre.

As a medical student, Chater was in a reserved occupation, but a number of his schoolmates were killed in France, the Battle of Britain had been fought literally over southern England, and after two years of medicine, he decided he had to join up. He left Cambridge and joined the Royal Navy as an ordinary seaman. It never occurred to Chater to try for a commission in any of the services, despite his classic "officer material" background. He has never sought or accepted responsibility, he says, "except when I'm working in the theatre".

Gordon Chater deliberately downplays his years in the RN during the Second World War. All he says when pressed is that he saw only ninety minutes' hard action from start to finish. Yet when one looks at his record closely, it represents three years of almost continuous service in dangerous waters. His commanding officer on one minesweeper was Nicholas Monsarrat, author of *The Cruel Sea*. Later he served on the Tobruk run in the Mediterranean. At the end of the war, he managed to get posted to Singapore. He was in Singapore when the signal came through for his demobilisation and decided to spend his four weeks demob leave in Australia, arriving in Fremantle aboard HMS *Swiftsure*.

His decision to settle in Australia (he was by then twenty-four) does not seem to have been a conscious one. When he applied for his demobilisation leave, his first choice of port had in fact been Shanghai, where his mother was born. However, the ship for Perth left first and Australia was where he ended up. He arrived with an introduction to Kathleen Robertson at the Minerva Theatre in Sydney. The long grey war was over, the sun was shining, and he was eating steak and eggs twice a day — an incredible luxury after years of wartime rationing and mess cooking.

Chater arrived in Sydney in July 1946. Kathleen Robertson, after he auditioned at the Minerva, offered him a part in *Dangerous Corner*, and an understudy role in *Love in Idleness* that were to tour New Zealand in October. In the meantime, he took a room in Elizabeth Bay for £2 a week and got a job washing dishes at the notorious "Hasty Tasty" hamburger joint in King's Cross, on the midnight to dawn shift. This enabled him to spend the day looking for work and attending more auditions.

Apart from the New Zealand tour, work did not come quickly. In those days, almost all the work for actors in Sydney was on radio. Chater called on Jean Hawkes (who was casting at 2GB) every Friday for "God knows how many weeks" before she took pity on him and gave him his first radio role in a series called "On Stage", with Neva Carr Glynn and Babs Mayhew.

Other radio work followed and also the odd job at the Minerva. "When somebody was drunk or they couldn't cast, I would get the role, which has been the story of my life." He started to make a name for himself as a character actor. In 1950, he picked up his first running part, a fifty-two-week contract on the "Roy Rene Radio Show" at £5 a week, playing a funny French waiter opposite "Mo" himself.

This was followed by three years' work for J. C. Williamson's in English comedies. *Worm's Eye View* ran for eighteen months and then followed *Seagulls Over Sorrento*, which also ran for more than a year. Both these plays were directed by William Hodge. In 1953, there was a trip back to England to see his family. His father died while he was there. In his final years, Chater's father did come to accept that his son was seriously engaged in an appropriate career. Chater derives wry satisfaction from the knowledge that his own estate will be several times larger than his father's.

In 1954, a new phase of Chater's career commenced with a series of revues staged by the new Phillip Street Theatre. Here his talents as an extraordinarily gifted character actor and mimic bloomed. It was also the start of a sometimes tempestuous working relationship with William Orr, the director of the theatre.

When the Phillip Street Theatre opened with *Top of the Bill* in 1954, there were three principals and a number of "also-rans". The three principals — Chater, Bud Tingwell and Margo Lee — were paid £5 a week each. The rest of the cost got £2. The next revue was a six-hander and all were paid £15. It ran for fifty-eight weeks and the cast had its salary doubled halfway through the run.

Following the long revue, Chater played in Lewis and Sybil Casson's Australian tour of *The Chalk Garden* in 1958. He then went back to England for a year. He did some television work there but after a few months was forced to take work as a barman in a pub. His mother refused to assist Chater, despite her comfortable circumstances: "No, no, you know what your father was like; if you go into the theatre you must never be supported in any way at all." He was rescued from a bar in London (where he was working) by a request from William Orr that he return immediately to Sydney. He returned on the same plane as the revue writer John McKellar, also summoned back from London by Orr. It was the last time Chater ever flew tourist; he woke up between San Francisco and Honolulu to find his head in a nun's lap. "Looking up at her I thought there'd been a crash and I was in heaven."

Back in Sydney, Chater was whisked into the Phillip Street revue *Hey Diddle Diddle*, which played through most of 1959. He was then cast in a musical based on Molière's comedies, *Mistress Money*, written for Chater by John McKellar and Dot Mendoza. While rehearsing, he went to a gala opening at the Phillip Street Theatre which precipitated his famous encounter with Bill Orr. The opening was a preview of a show Phillip Street was about to send on tour (its first attempt in this direction). Chater didn't like what he saw.

"It was indescribable. They were sending out work we had done with no regard for topicality, immediacy or even wit. They had in fact just chosen, higgledy-piggledy, things anybody could do. I was worried that this kind of thing was going to represent the legend that we had created."

At the party afterwards, the Chairman of the Phillip Street Theatre board, the lawyer John Kerr — later Governor-General — asked Chater his views about the show. Chater obliged at some length, and Kerr relayed the criticism to director William Orr. Orr, furious, approached Chater who was drinking champagne with friends and demanded that Chater confirm the criticism he had passed on to Kerr. Reluctantly, Chater confirmed that he thought it a bad revue, poorly directed. Orr's reaction, one of blind anger, resulted in a glass being smashed into Chater's face. The glass shattered and his face was very badly cut.

If this was not enough, within a week his right arm was paralysed, a reaction from a tetanus shot. The accident took place just over a week before Chater was due to open in his new show. On the opening night of *Mistress Money*, whenever it was necessary for Chater and Sheila Bradley (his co-star) to embrace, Bradley had to lift

Making his name as a comedy star, Sydney, 1960s (News Ltd)

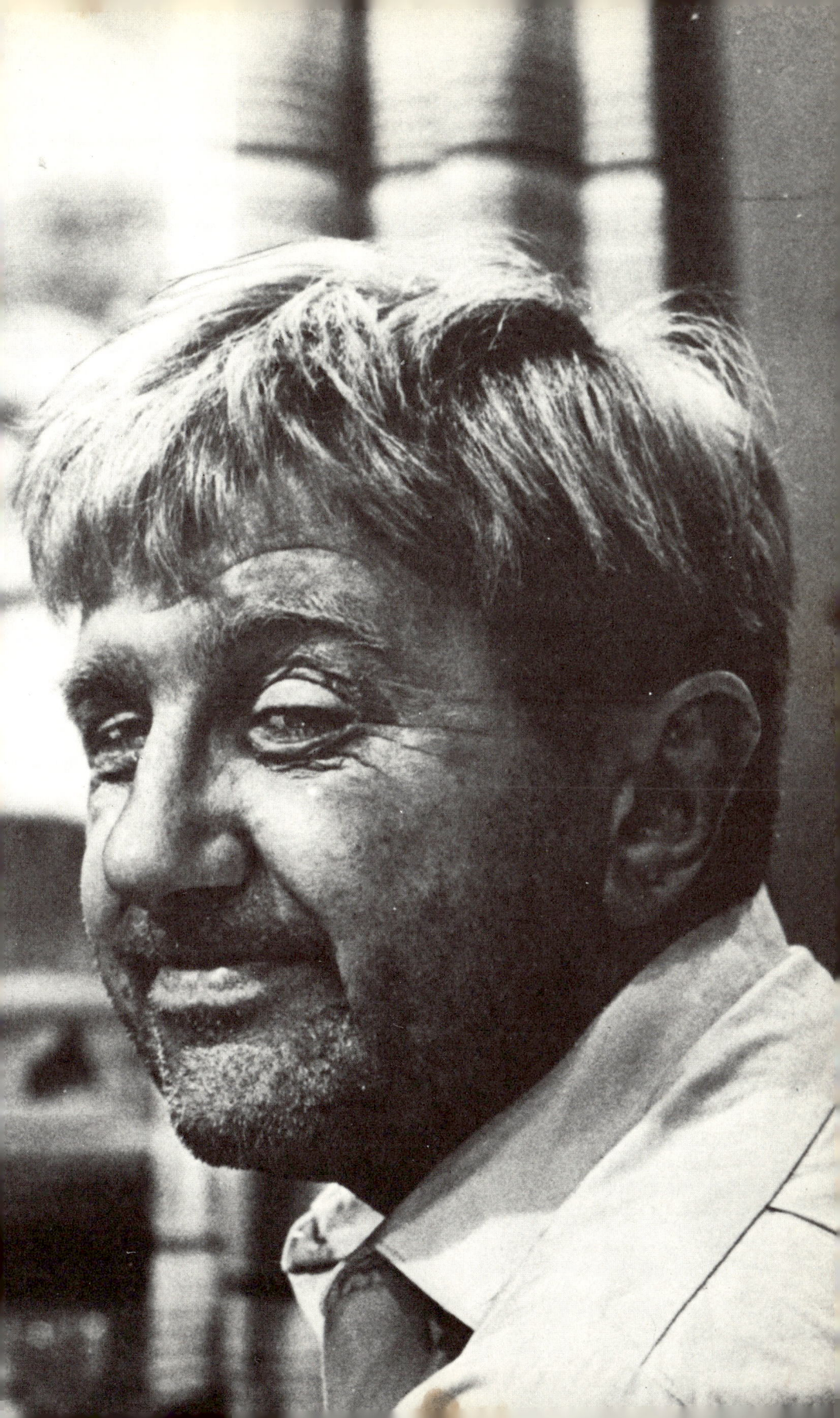

his useless arm and place it round her body. The plastic surgeons got rid of one facial scar but another remains, adding to the patina of Chater's worn but nobly mobile visage.

Naturally there were lawsuits. At the time, Chater was having a bad time getting work and he had no money. Finally, the case was settled out of court. Bill Orr paid him £1000, met some medical bills and they agreed to forget the whole matter. Chater was forced to work as a drama coach to support himself during this period and it was a very bleak time for him. It did not end until 1960, when Neil Hutchinson, manager of the Elizabethan Theatre Trust, decided to do an Australian production of *Charlie's Aunt*, the famous Victorian farce, and cast Chater in the feature part.

Feeling his oats after his enforced period of inactivity, Chater demanded billing as big as and above the title of the play — a totally outrageous demand never made before anywhere in the world by any actor who had played this part, including John Gielgud. It was, however, readily met by the Elizabethan Theatre Trust who were no doubt happy to agree to anything to avoid paying a high fee for the performance.

However, he was not destined to enjoy this spectacular billing for very long. The day *Charlie's Aunt* opened in Sydney, he was asked to fly to Toronto to appear in *The Duenna* in a part he had played in Australia. The Toronto season was to be a try-out for a New York season. Neil Hutchinson offered to release Chater from his contract if he could come up with a satisfactory actor to replace him in *Charlie's Aunt*. Chater offered the part to his old chum from *Seagulls Over Sorrento*, William Hodge. The day after Hodge took over the part, Chater received word that his mother had died in London. It was Christmas Eve 1960 and he was due to start rehearsals for *The Duenna* in Toronto on 1 January.

Problems awaited Chater in the Toronto version of *The Duenna*. He realised too late that only a Jewish actor could play a joke Jewish character like Isaac Mendoza in North America. Although it went over well with the early audiences, one prominent critic Nathan Cohen asked "... why Mr Chater has to give us such a disgusting, revolting, anti-Semitic joke of a performance". The play closed after three weeks.

Slightly battered by this experience, Chater, after seeing a few plays in New York, flew to London to settle his mother's affairs. She had spent her declining years in some comfort as a permanent guest at the Dudley Hotel, where for £15 a week she enjoyed the convenience of her own room and bathroom as well as a tiny sitting-room.

The Dudley Hotel, says Chater, was a uniquely English establishment, "very 'Separate Tables'". Chater called on one of his mother's great friends at the hotel, a Mrs Hamilton-Slee, to inquire about her last hours.

"Oh", she said, "your mother had been to a matinée at the Theatre Royal and she came in about five o'clock, and I said, 'Mrs Chater you look a little tired. I wouldn't bother changing for dinner tonight'. Your mother said she would rather die than not change for dinner — and did."

One last task awaited Chater before his mother's affairs could be finalised. In her will, Mrs Chater specified that she would like Chater to scatter her ashes from the Palace Pier at Brighton. So one cold and blustery March day, Chater picked up his mother from the funeral parlour and (fortified by several martinis) set out for the exposed Palace Pier.

"I tried the top level, then the lower levels, where the fishermen sit with their drooping moustaches and cloth caps, and finally I saw some arthritic old lady with blue hair getting out of a deckchair and I practically threw her out of the way and pushed my way to the rail and threw out the maternal ashes. As I did, the wind changed and they all blew back over one of these fishermen who looked up and said, 'What the fuckin' 'ell's that?' and I found it irresistable to say, 'It's me fuckin' muvver'."

Chater had come into a bit of money when his mother died so he took his aunt, the impecunious wife of a deceased admiral, for a trip to New York on the old *Queen Elizabeth*. Looking after the eccentric English aunt in New York was a difficult job. At the New Weston Hotel where they were staying, she commanded the black elevator attendant to "stop the lift" when it was a metre off the ground and loudly announced, "I've never had to be confined with niggers before". After a week, the aunt was packed off to Montreal and Chater returned to Sydney on the maiden voyage of the *Canberra* which sailed from the West Coast of the United States. In Sydney, nothing had changed. The Phillip Street Theatre urgently needed his talents on the bill after the first revue in their new theatre had flopped.

I saw Gordon Chater in most of his Phillip Street appearances. I particularly remember this one as a collection of thin sketches and slender lyrics saved from oblivion only by the sheer exuberance and skill of Chater's performance. This was too often the case at the Phillip Street Theatre, in my view: poor writing and traffic-cop direction rescued by extraordinary individual performances.

Yes Please was followed by other revues. None of them was actually directed by Bill Orr. Their dispute had been patched up, more or less, but there was no suggestion that they would ever work together again.

In 1964, Chater was asked by an old friend, Ormsby Wilkins, the news director of 2UE, if he would like a radio programme for an hour every morning. It was to be "an hour of yak", for which he was paid £100 a week. As a radio "personality", Chater was asked to a party at Fairwater, the residence of Warwick and Mary Fairfax, which fronts Seven Shilling Beach between Double Bay and Point Piper in Sydney's Eastern Suburbs.

The Fairfaxes had thrown their home open as a benefit for the Metropolitan Opera auditions, a cause close to Mary Fairfax's heart. Chater could not wait to see this house, "I've never tripped over so much jade in my life", and he got on rather well with Mary Fairfax. Mary asked him to leave the hoi polloi and join Warwick for a glass of sherry. It was a very important glass of sherry. Warwick liked Chater's work at the Phillip Street Theatre and believed it would convert well to television. Did Chater agree? Chater murmured agreement and Warwick announced that he would contact the legendary Rupert Henderson — head of the Fairfax media group.

ATN-7 Sydney, the Fairfax television station, arranged for Chater to meet Carol Ray, whom he remembered as an English musical comedy star of the early 1940s. Carol suggested to Chater a show like "That Was the Week that Was" — a famous weekly revue on British television. Barry Creyton, the third member of the trio, was engaged and rehearsals started, only to come to a grinding halt a few days later when Chater decided things were heading for disaster. There was no real script and he felt nobody associated with the project was capable of producing one.

He saw Rupert Henderson and explained that the pilot needed to be prepared properly. Henderson agreed to all requests. Was there, Henderson asked, anybody in Australia sufficiently experienced to supervise the project? Chater recommended Michael Plant; he had just returned to Australia and had the wit and the experience needed.

In May 1964, the pilot of "The Mavis Bramston Show", after eight weeks of intensive work by the team, was produced in the 2GB auditorium. The Fairfax management was very pleased. Henderson particularly liked the custard-pie sequences.

It was decided to begin the series with six episodes starting at the beginning of November 1964. If the initial six did well, a larger number would be ordered for the following year. Chater was to get

Publicising the London production of *The Elocution of Benjamin Franklin*, 1978 (News Ltd)

£150 a show for twelve shows even if only six were made.

"The Mavis Bramston Show" was a tremendous success from day one. It gave a new dimension to what could be done in the way of local production. The early influences on Australian television production were American. Often the very worst of American producers would shuffle into Sydney or Melbourne with their well-worn concepts and their lacklustre formats to an undiscriminating, almost credulous welcome. "Bramston" was a break with that Yankee hand-me-down mentality. It was a watershed for advertisers too. They found that advertising was actually profitable in a programme featuring Australian performers who could also be seen in the flesh when not performing. They were real. Were the people on the box from Hollywood real too? They never would be quite so real after "The Mavis Bramston Show".

Chater, though already well known in the limited world of the theatre, now bloomed into a national celebrity. In February 1965, he was asked to dine with Rupert Henderson at the Chelsea in King's Cross in Sydney, a restaurant then famous for (among other things) the amount of old silver lying about on its tables. Chater remembers insisting on Australian wine rather than the expensive Pouilly-Fuissé.

Rupert Henderson offered to double Chater's fee per show. Chater wouldn't hear of it as it would have involved a breach of contract. A puzzled Henderson agreed he would nominate the salary in the new contract and laughed when Chater said, "I know you won't insult me". Rupert Henderson drove Chater back to his little terrace house close to the city in Paddington.

But the night was far from over. Chater asked Henderson in for a brandy and he ended staying until after two, talking about his relationship with the Fairfax family. He spoke of them warmly and with considerable affection. He acknowledged the opportunities the Fairfaxes had given him, what they had taught him about art, fine wines and the art of living graciously. The upshot of this strange evening was that Chater and Rupert Henderson became firm friends.

Henderson and he had only one row and that was about Gwen Plumb. Henderson wanted her dropped from the finale of an episode of "Bramston" and Chater stuck to his guns and his friend "Gwennie". Compromise was achieved when Miss Plumb agreed to modify the strapless costume that was the centre of the dispute. Henderson was mollified and his avuncular relationship with Chater continued. Chater exploited his special relationship with Henderson to increase the budget for his show. "Oh, come on, Uncle Rupert, open up the purse strings, don't be so mean" became a favourite appeal, and the good-natured impertinence never failed.

Gordon Chater was to be a contract artist for ATN for four years. After "Bramston" finished, he was the star of the successful series "My Name's McGooley". Finally, to work out his contract, he agreed to do a show called "The Gordon Chater Show" about which he prefers not to talk. When he left ATN after those four years, he received a letter from Rupert Henderson in which he apologised for the failure of the ATN management to back up his marvellous successes in "Bramston" and "McGooley" with every resource at its disposal.

Harry Miller snapped Chater up for a play as soon as he left ATN. It was called *You Know I Can't Hear You When the Water's Running* and opened to ecstatic press notices, but it was not able to survive the rolling effects of a petrol strike followed within days by both a transport strike and a postal strike.

The next seven years were slow for Chater. He was no longer a young actor. His television work had typed him as a specialist in larger-than-life comedy roles. He had never been handsome enough to play leading men. Despite these limitations, the biggest problem must have been (although he is too polite to say so) that the theatrical

In *The Elocution of Benjamin Franklin*, Sydney, 1984 (Peter Holderness)

world in Australia is miniscule. The better known an actor gets in the Australian theatre, the more he cuts his own throat.

There was a big revue at the Chevron Hotel in Sydney in 1972 called *The Mavis McMahon Show* directed by James Fishburn. It was the show in which Gary MacDonald made his debut. There was a longish run in *Scandals of '74* again at the Chevron. In 1975, he appeared in *Jockey Club Stakes* with Robert Coote and Wilfrid Hyde White. Chater describes this tour (David Frost's first theatrical production) as a superb production but a marketing disaster.

The tour ended in the red, and David Frost's Australian associates had to pay Chater the $5000 they owed him out of the success they enjoyed with a tour by singer Neil Diamond. When that cheque finally turned up, Chater walked it straight over to Qantas and asked for "a *chaise longue* round the world please".

By this time, however, Chater, having learnt the lessons of the past, was a good deal more financially secure. A shrewd property investor, he had made money from his houses in Sydney at Paddington and Palm Beach. He had come into some money when his mother died and more after the death of his sister. His stockbroker, Arthur Hordern, had over the years made more wise than foolish suggestions and bachelor Chater was not burdened with the costly obligations of feeding and dressing a wife, and schooling and straightening the teeth of his offspring.

So, unlike many actors, by the middle 1970s he was comfortably well off. But he wanted still to work and stage work was slow in coming. In November 1975, Chater approached Phillip Ashton, the owner of the Royal Hotel at Paddington, and offered to take over his Elephant Bar which had just opened. The week before Chater took over, it had taken $300. Within a couple of months under Chater's management, the takings rose to $3000 a week.

Chater was particularly amused by a lot of the publicity that followed, which suggested that he was working in a pub because he was broke. Inaccurate as it all was, it did have the effect of letting the world know the address of his bar. Gwen Plumb summed it up by saying he was simply getting paid for doing what he normally did for nothing at his house in Palm Beach.

His job at the Elephant Bar ended in a typically Australian manner. He was injured when he tried to separate a couple of brawling drunks. He tore ligaments in a leg and for a while was supported by that fine old Australian institution, workers' compo. After he recovered, he accepted a lucrative offer to open a restaurant in the Palace Hotel in Perth. Chater was given a free apartment, full expenses and ten per cent of the gross takings. He did well. "We were doing 300 at lunch and 500 at dinner."

Before going to Perth early in 1976, Chater was offered the sole role in *The Elocution of Benjamin Franklin*. He rather warily told Hilary Linstead, his agent, that he was interested. "Well I really thought I had given up the theatre, but this was a wonderful play." He did insist on plenty of time to plan, learn and rehearse, and he also insisted that he be allowed to tour it commercially if it was successful at the Nimrod Theatre. All Chater's requirements were met. It was agreed rehearsals would start as soon as he got back from Perth.

The play was a hit the moment it opened. Its six-week season was entirely sold out at the tiny Nimrod Theatre within thirty-six hours. It was moved to the 700-seat Glebe Arts Theatre. It then toured

Australia, played in London and finally was taken to America, opening in San Francisco and then playing in a small theatre off-Broadway.

The Elocution of Benjamin Franklin deals with a subject that makes many people uneasy: pederasty. It is to many one of the basest manifestations of sexuality. The sole character on stage in *Benjamin* is an overweight, aging, reluctant transvestite, Robert O'Brien, who is charged with the task of teaching elocution to the twelve-year-old Benjamin, who is never seen on stage.

O'Brien sees his affection for Benjamin as being parental. The precocious Benjamin, who has already seduced another adult, is now determined to seduce the pathetic O'Brien. He resists. He has his ethics. Despite his propriety, society in the end wreaks a horrible fate on him. The play opens with O'Brien naked. For the rest of the performance he is clothed, but there is a sense of nakedness that remains. It's a device designed to create a sense of vulnerability from the start, and it probably would not have worked in the hands (or should one say body) of an actor of lesser skill.

Chater is philosophic about his success in *Benjamin*. He says he was, as usual, the third actor to be offered the part. The author, Steven Spears, sent it first to Frank Thring, who does not even remember receiving it. He is also amused that the American producer, James Hammerstein, who saw the play in Australia and decided to produce it in America, wanted to set it in Atlanta and use an American actor with a southern accent. Fortunately, Stephen Sondheim and Hal Prince saw the show and convinced Hammerstein to leave it alone. There was, they said, no performance without Chater. The *New York Times* seems to have agreed with Sondheim and Prince. Mel Gussow noted acidly at the end of a generally favourable review, that, in fact, "the evening exists because of the inventiveness of Mr Chater".

There were, however, a few anxious moments on the way to New York. The season in San Francisco nearly failed. The producers had hoped that the large homosexual community there would support it but Chater was skeptical about this. The play was, he felt, too depressing for most homosexuals. It was only the more sophisticated ones who would wish to see it — not the great hordes from Castro Street — and indeed, despite excellent notices, the play opened to empty houses. It was saved by the energies of the theatre's press agent, a "wonderful little German-American called Hans Kolmar". Kolmar rang all the critics who had given the play such good reviews and told them that despite the reviews, the notice of closure was already up. He persuaded them to come out strongly in the media and ask San Francisco to support the play to demonstrate that the city could sustain innovative conceptual theatre and not merely subscription theatre and touring companies. It worked. Within three days, Chater was playing to full houses.

Chater's New York performance in 1978 won him an "Obie", an annual award given for off-Broadway productions. He was also fortunate in that several of the people connected with the New York production were attorneys, one of them an immigration specialist. Because of this, Chater obtained his "green card" (which all non-Americans who wish to live and work in America must have) without a great deal of difficulty or delay. It was probably the green card more than anything else which decided Chater to stay in New York.

He had made quite a lot of money out of *Benjamin*. This, added to his Australian stocks, gave him a certain measure of independence. He was by this time in his late fifties and felt he should be easing up a little. He said in an interview in 1982: "I am now nearly sixty and winding down. And this is the most perfect place to wind down. If I wish, I can go to the theatre all the time."

He was, however, far from finished. There was a part in the Molière play *The Learned Lady* at the Roundabout Theatre, a small company but with an incredible 26,000 subscribers. There was a number of other off-Broadway and out-of-town parts, and then *Whodunit* on Broadway. Chater is happy to play in a touring company in America. The cast is properly treated with ample travelling allowances and accommodations.

In 1981, he returned to Australia to play in *The Dresser* with Warren Mitchell and Ruth Cracknell. In New York in 1982, he declined the part of the Major-General in the post-D'Oyley Carte production of *The Pirates of Penzance* — "I don't think I could have got up each morning knowing I had to sing that song in double-time each night!"

Chater is still living in the spare room of the man who played his stand-by when he came to New York to do *Benjamin*. It is close to the restaurants and theatres of the fashionable midtown district. He is an assiduous correspondent and keeps in touch with his many old friends. Barely a day goes by without Chater writing at least one letter to Australia, and he is very hospitable to old friends who visit New York. One of his oldest friends is the Australian novelist and playwright Sumner Locke Elliott who has lived in New York since 1948 and who performed with Chater at the old Minerva Theatre in 1947.

As this book was going to press, Gordon Chater was back in Australia for a few months touring *The Elocution of Benjamin Franklin*, with the possibility of a film being made of the play. Chater has said he is happy to be in an Australian film that is not "one of those costume things".

It is a long journey from an English public school to an apartment in Manhattan. Though he grew up elsewhere, almost all of his adult, working life has been spent in Australia, and it is difficult to think of him as anything but Australian. Nonetheless, it is interesting to note that, now an expatriate, his relationship with this country remains a mutually warm and affectionate one.

It is perhaps significant that this distinguishes him from some of his native-born equivalents who spent their childhoods here. Many of these are far more ambivalent about "home".

GRAHAM FRASER

Although the media give a different impression, few of the Australians who live in America are actors, writers, opera singers — or drug dealers. Most of them are ordinary civilians. Sumner Locke Elliott, the Australian author, has said that you run into people from Dubbo *everywhere*. This is the story of somebody from Cooma.

By the time this is published, Graham Fraser's collection of Chinese and Japanese art will have arrived at, and been displayed by, the Art Gallery of New South Wales. Fraser himself may briefly become a celebrity. The collection Graham Fraser is placing in the Sydney gallery represents the *crème de la crème* of his activities over the last seven years. His collection has been acquired without the aid of any inherited capital or formal art training. It has been financed by gains from the sale of other pieces. Fraser is a respected expert in the tiny but highly competitive world of Chinese art dealers and collectors.

He was born in 1937 in Cooma, his family having been graziers in the district since 1832. The original family property is now under the waters of Lake Eucumbene. His father's property, Glenwood, was not large — about 420 hectares with another 400 hectares of leased pasture — and carried sheep and a few head of cattle.

Fraser had two brothers and two sisters. Until he was nine his schooling was by correspondence, supervised by his mother. After that it was a nine-kilometre bike ride each way to the Rocky Plains Public School, a traditional one-room affair with about a dozen students. He went to high school on the coast, at Bega, boarding with other kids from the southern portion of the State at a Bega hostel. Fraser, who has never studied art or design, concentrated on agricultural courses, assuming his future lay on the land.

At sixteen, Fraser passed his Intermediate Certificate and left school to work at Glenwood. He did the normal things a son does on his father's patch of dirt, trapping rabbits, fixing fences and shearing sheep. The first inkling of any artistic temperament appeared when he started wool-classing. He was almost instinctively able to distinguish the different textures. Neighbours soon started asking him to class their own wool.

Glenwood, however, was too small to support all the Frasers. The Snowy Scheme was under construction in 1956 so Graham Fraser

---

Graham Fraser, United States, 1984 (Serlin Studios)

took a construction job on the Lake Eucumbene project, for the New South Wales Public Works Department as a timekeeper. After eight months, he lost the job when an American contractor took over from the Public Works Department.

By this time, Fraser, still living at home, had become engaged to Diana Locker, a girl from a nearby property. He was able to marry Diana when he got a job as a salesman for the Singer Sewing Machine Company. They moved to a house in Cooma. Graham and Diana Fraser had two children, a son Roderick, and a daughter Vicki-Anne. The marriage eventually collapsed after five years.

In the years before he left the Cooma district for Sydney, Fraser became a representative for Legal & General, an insurance company he joined after he left Singer in 1960. A natural salesman, he became a member of the elite Millionaires' Club, a worldwide association of very successful insurance salesmen. His financial troubles arose when he opened a nightclub in the Victorian border town of Corryong, designed to attract the 14,000 men working the Snowy projects in that area. The club, optimistically called El Dorado, proved a financial disaster, swallowing his savings and plunging him heavily into debt. It was in the detritus of El Dorado that his marriage finally expired.

"I was spending too much time away. I was busy with all these different things and had all these financial problems. That's what caused the end of it."

In 1965, aged twenty-seven, having made arrangements with his wife for the care of their children, he left Cooma — first for Canberra, which failed to meet his expectations, and a few weeks later, Sydney. Sydney was a fresh start, away from the broken marriage, the pressing debts of the failed Alpine nightclub, and a family property too small to support all the children.

In Sydney Fraser joined up with a Canadian and went into the door-to-door business, selling stainless-steel cookware. He took a tiny studio flat at Point Piper with a breathtaking harbour view. The door-to-door sales operation lasted a year. His next venture gave him the first hint that perhaps his wool-classing ability was not just an accidental talent and that he had some natural artistic antenna not shared by everybody.

Sitting in a King's Cross coffee shop one night, Fraser observed a man selling drawings of Paddington terrace houses. He felt instinctively they were good and asked the artist how they were selling. He established they were selling badly, largely because they were seriously overpriced. The artist was attempting to get $60 for a pencil study, which Fraser thought was a ridiculous price to ask, especially outside a coffee shop in King's Cross. He arranged for the artist to have the drawings silkscreened and then got them framed simply in plain wood.

Fraser sold the silkscreened drawings to department stores and jewellers — in Sydney at first and later in the country. Small ones were sold at $10, large ones at $15. Fraser's arrangement with the artist, Kevin (his last name has vanished into the fog of time), was that all first orders would be split fifty-fifty, with Fraser getting seventy-five per cent of all second orders. All further reorders went to the artist. The venture netted Fraser enough to finance a trip to London. A South African girl he had met in Sydney had moved there and he was keen to see her. At this stage, Fraser had no thought of making a career outside Australia.

He sailed for London at the end of 1967, aged thirty, aboard the *Fairsea* and was surprised to find how little money he had left by the time he arrived in Britain.

A few weeks after he arrived, he met a mortgage-broker at a party and asked if he could work for him for nothing, to learn the tricks of the trade. After three months learning the ropes, supplementing dwindling resources with the odd commission cheque, Fraser found a tiny office with French furniture in Sackville Street for £5 a week. He registered two company names for ten shillings each, Fraser Finance & Mortgages, and City & Provincial Finance Company. Expensive business cards and letterheads were printed and Fraser prepared to enter the fringe banking business.

His venture into mortgage banking, however, began at the very moment the government applied a severe squeeze to the credit markets. Nobody had money to lend, and those that did had to charge such high rates that nobody could afford to borrow it. Things were looking pretty gloomy for the young Australian mortgage banker when he was introduced to Jacqueline Killearn, the glamorous widow of Miles Lampson, the famous British diplomat, who had become Lord Killearn when he was appointed to the peerage.

Fraser moved into a wing of Lady Killearn's country house in Sussex, although he still maintained his London apartment. Jackie Killearn took him about with her and introduced him to a variety of interesting people under the most auspicious circumstances. Fraser persuaded Jackie Killearn that her manor house was a losing proposition when managed as a stately house, open to the public for a fee. He felt it would do better as a working farm, and supervised the necessary alterations.

When Jackie Killearn asked Fraser to quietly sell the large collection of Chinese art she had inherited from her husband, she probably did not realise the new direction she was pointing him in was one from which he was not to deviate. The collection had been acquired by her husband during his diplomatic service in China many years earlier. Fraser complained that he knew nothing of Chinese art. She suggested he use a Christie's valuation she had obtained to fix minimum prices for each piece.

The arrangement between Fraser and Lady Killearn was that he would keep everything over the Christie's valuation for all pieces he sold. By selling the collection piecemeal, she was able to avoid Christie's commissions and the publicity that goes with the sale of a well-known collection. With his mortgage banking business in Sackville Street in the doldrums, Fraser decided to try it.

The collection was large and Fraser started off in nearby Brighton with a few small pieces, asking fifty per cent above the Christie's valuation. To his utter surprise, the Brighton dealers paid without a murmur. The success rate continued. Fraser started taking pieces to other dealers in the district and eventually to London. Doubling the Christie's valuation did not seem to affect the eagerness of the dealers to buy. He did not become suspicious until, about three months after he had started, he went to a sale at Sotheby's, attempting to learn more about the market. He was surprised to see several pieces he had sold to dealers up for sale, and horrified when dishes he had sold for £25 based on the Christie's valuation were knocked down for £1500 each. The man Christie's sent to do the valuation for Lady Killearn had walked into her house and, running up against more apparently high-class ceramics than he had seen in his life before, decided they were all fakes, and quietly valued them as such. Even after Fraser had doubled his prices, he was still selling at vastly under the true value. By the time he realised this, he had sold the bulk of the collection. The remaining pieces were, however, sold at very different prices, and to more important dealers. In this way, Fraser acquired an amount of capital and a little knowledge of who was who in the business.

One dealer he first met when he was disposing of the Killearn collection, with whom he still does much business, was the Italian Guiseppi Eskenazi who operates through galleries in London, Milan and Zurich. Fraser calls Eskenazi the world's leading dealer in Oriental art. He also met a girl called Shirley Day who worked for Marchant's in London, who was to teach him the nuts and bolts of Chinese art.

He met Shirley while he was still selling pieces for Lady Killearn.

With brother (centre), mother and sisters on the family property, Glenwood, 1957

He was in Marchant's one day selling something and Shirley went past on her way out to lunch. As she went past Fraser she whispered, "Don't sell it". Fraser took her to lunch and ended up assisting her to start up as a dealer in her apartment in Chelsea. She sold some of the Killearn pieces for him and he financed her opening stock. She and Fraser became very close and he was constantly in her company when he was in London.

However, when he was not in London he was still spending a lot of time with Jackie Killearn, and he was also seeing several other women as well. This finally ended his relationship with both Shirley Day and Jackie Killearn. He was also flying around Europe with a well-connected Iranian called Farah.

Shirley Day is today one of London's best-known dealers and is possibly the leading one *anywhere* in Japanese art. She taught Fraser, a fast learner, the ins and outs of the London salerooms. She acquainted him with the old dealers' trick of buying and reselling quickly before paying for the purchase. To do this successfully requires an excellent knowledge of market value. In the securities market this is called arbitrage, and is an occupation strictly for professionals.

His commission to sell Lady Killearn's collection was finished but Fraser was now hooked on the art market and on Chinese ceramics in particular. One of his first buys, at Sotheby's, was a Japanese Kakiemon jar from the seventeenth century. For this Fraser paid £1200, to the consternation of Shirley Day, but two weeks later he resold to a Japanese dealer for £2700. He also found in Phillip's saleroom a Japanese Kutani vase from the seventeenth century, which he got for £50 and sold within days for £1000.

Fraser was selling only to dealers using Shirley's flat as an office and maintaining a separate residence in Montpelier Square in Knightsbridge. The process of educating himself included endless visits to the British and the Victoria and Albert Museums where he thoroughly familiarised himself with their various Chinese ceramics collections. He also acquired an expensive collection of out-of-print books and catalogues, containing illustrations of old collections. The skills that first surfaced when he started wool-classing were now fully developed. The instinctive recognition of characteristic texture and design seems to have been there from the start. Once he had studied an original, or a good illustration of one, Fraser was almost always able to spot other examples immediately if he came across them.

These, however, are the skills of scholarship alone. The real training for a dealer takes place in the salerooms, and London was the ideal place for this, being the headquarters of both Christie's and Sotheby's. Closely examining a piece before a sale and then watching it go to auction was the practical training Fraser obtained in London.

After two years of education and dealing in London, Fraser was anxious to test new territory. With this in view and partly to get away from the English winter, he took a trip to Lisbon where, ensconced in his hotel suite, he checked the telephone directory for dealers in Oriental art. In this fashion he found a man called Popper who specialised in the sale of Oriental rugs but handled art pieces on the side. He had a dozen on display at a hotel in Estoril. Fraser went to have a look and found them all to be T'ang. The price tags seemed to have too many zeros for him though, until he discovered they were written in Portuguese escudos.

To the delight of Mr Popper, who had not adjusted his price for fourteen years, Fraser brought all twelve pieces. He then called Guiseppi Eskenazi in Milan, knowing he was actively searching for T'ang pieces. The Italian dealer flew to Lisbon that day and purchased all twelve pieces at ten times the price the luckless Mr Popper had obtained for them a few hours before.

Mr Popper, blissfully unaware that he was the beginning of a lucrative daisychain, continued to supply Fraser with Chinese art from time to time from his extensive private collection. Over the space of three years, Fraser made about nine trips to Lisbon. It was one of these Lisbon trips that eventually resulted in Fraser moving the base of his operations to California.

He was having drinks in the bar at the Ritz Hotel in Lisbon one day and got into conversation with an American couple who, as Americans do, asked him what he did for a living. Fraser said he dealt in Chinese art. The Americans announced they knew where there was a lot of *that*. It turned out that the couple, from California, had seen hundreds of pieces of Chinese ceramics stacked in the basement of Scripps College, at Claremont, which is just outside Los Angeles.

A few months later, in April 1971, Fraser flew to California to investigate the supposed cache. To his surprise he discovered his drinking companions had not been exaggerating. He found 400 pieces of Chinese ceramics and about twenty bronzes lying unattended and uncatalogued in the basement of Scripps College. It proved extraordinarily difficult to locate the actual owner of the collection. After two weeks, the college coyly admitted they did not actually own the collection, that it was the property of an alumnus who had died, and was on loan to them.

The late owner of the collection was one William Bacon Pettus and Fraser discovered he had been buried in the Temple of the Chimes, in Berkeley, California. After a couple of calls to the mortuary office he was able to track down the next of kin and eventually found himself talking to Mr Pettus's son in Lafayette, Louisiana. He told him his father's collection was lying in the basement gathering dust and that the college had no intentions of displaying it. There had been breakages. There would be more. He offered Pettus $50,000. Pettus flew to Claremont the next day and accepted the deal subject to the college picking ten pieces from the collection.

There were two problems with this deal. Fraser didn't have $50,000 and there were only six really good pieces in the collection. He was confident, however, that the man who was teaching Oriental art at Scripps would not be able to identify the really valuable ones. Fraser maintains that academics rarely can.

He was able to arrange finance in Los Angeles. Fraser took in a partner who provided $50,000 in return for half of all proceeds. The deal was finalised and the college expert failed to select any of the pieces that Fraser was interested in. Among the pieces he did not choose was a *famille rose* six-sided bowl from the Yung Cheng period. Though only an early eighteenth-century piece, this was crucially important because of the transitional characteristics it carried. Fraser describes the bowl as the most important one of its type ever seen.

Over a period of three years the Pettus Collection was gradually liquidated. Fraser estimates it fetched about $400,000. The *famille rose* bowl was sold by Sotheby's in April 1974 for US$238,000, of which his share was half for a capital investment of nothing.

This was the start of his shifting of activity to southern California, where he now spends most of his time. He has purchased other collections in the years since, as well as numbers of individual pieces. His comprehensive knowledge of who is interested in what varieties of Oriental art has enabled him to frequently take positions other buyers have hesitated to. His recent acquisition of the Hoover Collection is an example of how well he competes against the big boys.

This collection had belonged to the late President Hoover and came onto the market following the death of his daughter-in-law, Mrs Margaret Hoover, in 1982. It consisted of 200 pieces of porcelain, and included some important Ming and Kang Hsi pieces. Sotheby's had valued it — they had given both a high and low estimate to the executors of the estate — and expected to be given the job of auctioning it. Herbert Hoover Jr, grandson of the late president, was the principal executor of the estate, and Fraser wrote to him offering to meet the high value of the Sotheby's estimate for the collection. This was an attractive offer. Not only did it match the highest Sotheby's price on each piece, it guaranteed that all pieces would be sold and that there would be no shipping and storage expenses on unsold pieces. Moreover, it avoided the hefty Sotheby's commission while still providing the estate with an independent valuation.

The offer was subject to an examination of the collection, and this confirmed Fraser's view that Sotheby's had undervalued several of the more interesting pieces. His offer was accepted. Guiseppi Eskenazi flew from London and bought four pieces from the collection immediately.

Fraser now regrets selling one of the bowls from the collection to

Eskenazi. He would have liked to keep it for his own collection, which he did not really start until the late 1970s. However, this was one case where Eskenazi bested Fraser. Eskenazi subsequently priced the bowl at a quarter of a million dollars and it sold at that price without trouble.

Fraser bought three interesting pieces from Senator Hugh Scott, for many years Republican leader in the Senate. Scott was the author of the book *The Golden Age of Chinese Art*. This contained illustrations of a number of the pieces he owned, mostly T'ang. Fraser read the book, looked at the illustrations and decided that, in his view, the author did not really know the difference between his good and ordinary pieces.

Fraser visited the senator to see if he was interested in selling anything. Scott felt he had a good collection, containing about 400 pieces. Fraser says that, as with many American collections, size is no indication of quality. There were only two pieces in the collection Fraser really wanted. One was a T'ang silver stem cup, an example of which he had long been looking for, and the other a T'ang silver mirror.

The senator told Fraser he was thinking of selling a few pieces. He might sell the two Fraser wanted but would need $8500 for the cup and $14,000 for the mirror. To the senator's shock — he no doubt expected a certain amount of haggling — Fraser held out his hand and accepted the deal on the spot. When the senator asked him "how he wanted to handle this", Fraser told him that in his pocket were two cashier's cheques made out to Senator Scott for $10,000 each. Fraser would give him a personal cheque for the balance. The senator suddenly realised he had made a deal. "Oh my God, I guess I've sold these pieces."

The silver cup Fraser paid $8500 for, sold in Sotheby's in London for $32,000. The $14,000 mirror fetched $50,000. Later Fraser returned to see the senator. In his cabinet he had seen a small green pottery rhyton — a horn-shaped drinking vessel — from the T'ang period. He had assumed it was a fake the first time he visited the senator. Now he took it out and examined it in the light.

"I could see the iridescence and the fine crackling and I thought, 'This thing's absolutely genuine'. I asked him how much he wanted for it. He said $5000. I said, 'That'll be fine'. Actually it was better than I thought. When I got home and looked through some of my books I found the piece illustrated."

The piece had originally been in a Japanese museum up until the Second World War. The senator had travelled extensively throughout

China and Japan after the war — and had been given many gifts in the days before munificence towards elected officials was frowned upon. This had been one of them. The rhyton also went to Sotheby's and fetched slightly over $40,000.

Six months later Fraser called once more on the senator in Washington. By then Scott had studied his Sotheby's catalogues and seen the prices his pieces had brought. Politely he informed Fraser he did not think he should sell him anything further. In future he would deal direct with Sotheby's. Equally politely Fraser told the senator he didn't have anything left that was worth selling through Sotheby's. This actually turned out to be a little pessimistic. Scott did sell a few pieces at Sotheby's but they fetched nothing like the prices Fraser's three pieces had.

Another interesting figure that Fraser dealt with was a wealthy Santa Barbara resident, Wright Ludington. Fraser was looking through the Santa Barbara Museum one day and noticed a couple of interesting pieces marked as being on loan from Ludington, a famous art collector. Fraser knew the curator and asked him for Ludington's telephone number, but was told the museum was unable to release it. He managed to establish Ludington's address, however, and when he returned to Pasadena, where he was staying at the time, he wrote to him offering to buy the two pieces he had seen in the Santa Barbara Museum.

Both pieces were Sung period — eleventh century. One was a dish incised with a free design of flowers. The other a moulded dish which many people now consider to be the finest example of its type yet seen. In his letter to Ludington, Fraser offered $35,000 for the pair. Within the week the post brought a reply from Ludington asking him to Santa Barbara for lunch.

At lunch Wright Ludington confessed that he had completely forgotten the pieces. After a pleasant meal they drove to the Santa Barbara Museum where Fraser pointed them out. Ludington called for the cabinet to be opened, took out the two pieces and handed them to Fraser. Nothing further was said and Fraser realised the transaction had been completed. Fraser told Ludington he would send him a cheque within thirty days. Within seven days he had sold both pieces for $70,000.

In recent years, Fraser has added Chinese painting to his list of interests, in particular twentieth-century Chinese painting. He has also dealt in Japanese pieces although he still obtains second opinions in this area. In his principal field, Chinese ceramics, he has been happy to depend on his own judgement for many years now.

Graham Fraser's principal interest in the last six or seven years has been building his own collection. It now contains about forty pieces including paintings. It beings with the Han period and includes Sui and T'ang ceramics as well as a few Ming pieces.

"I have got a good many Chinese paintings. I certainly would have liked to have collected bronzes, early bronzes, but they are so rare, and you usually cannot find the quality you want. Probably the best-quality things I've got are the T'ang and the Sui."

Late in 1983, Fraser began looking for a home for that part of his collection he had stabilised. He looked for a place where it could go on permanent display and would be properly cared for by experts. And he wanted it to be in Australia, preferably in Sydney.

"Well, I was born in Australia and I would very much like some of my things to be there. They just don't have such pieces. The Sydney gallery is about to build a new section to house Asian art, but quite apart from the difficulties of raising funds to buy Asian pieces, they would find it very difficult to obtain good examples now."

Fraser's collection will fill a large gap in the Art Gallery of New South Wales' range. The National Gallery of Victoria has some excellent blue-and-white Ming, but little from earlier periods. The Fraser Collection includes not only examples, but good examples, of all major periods.

Now in his middle forties, Fraser is an active and virile man. However, he says he has grown accustomed to single life and is unlikely to marry again. He is not close to his children, who live in Australia, and will probably make separate arrangements for them in his will.

His interest in the Sydney collection will almost certainly increase as he gets older. I would not be surprised to see regular additions made to the collection and even the odd withdrawal as Graham Fraser finds more representative items. This assumes continuing interest by the New South Wales gallery in Asian art and an indication that it is prepared to continue investing in it. This seems likely since the present curator, Edmund Capon, is an expert on Chinese painting.

The collection may not become frozen until Graham Fraser dies. When he does, the only way he can ensure that his collection is not broken up and sold to the eager young beavers of the future is to leave it intact to the Trustees of the New South Wales gallery. In the meantime, the collection will remain technically his property which, given his knowledge and interest in this highly specialised market, can only be advantageous to the collection and to all who see it.

DAME JUDITH ANDERSON

One hundred and sixty kilometres north of Los Angeles, on what was in Spanish times called the Camino Real, and is now Highway 101, lies the city of Santa Barbara. It spills down the seaward slopes of the Los Padres National Forest to the waters of the Pacific Ocean. Between these modest mountains and ocean beaches nestles an enclave of gently rising foothills and fertile valleys. The hillsides are thick with avocado and the valleys with lemon and olive trees. The mesas and valleys are dotted with stables and riding trails, and simple cottages mingle with rococo Italianate and Spanish villas. In gardens the bent backs of Mexican workers are everywhere visible and the ear catches the programmed swirl of sprinklers dispensing precious water over manicured lawns and flowerbeds. Here Australian gums and ferns grow in imported profusion. Wattle, which now grows wild, is rooted out like a noxious weed.

Santa Barbara's climate is marred only by hazy mist in late spring and early summer. For the rest of the year, the sun shines with stolid regularity, setting each night in a kaleidoscopic burst of reds, yellows, purples and pinks as the dying rays strike clouds held captive over the ocean by the mountains looming from behind.

If you exit Highway 101 at the Montecito Inn — once owned by Charlie Chaplin and Fatty Arbuckle — and head towards the old Ronald Colman Ranch, where Winston Churchill wrote a portion of his memoirs and John and Jackie Kennedy dallied for their honeymoon before the days of the Second Camelot, you shortly arrive at Arbroath, the home of Dame Judith Anderson, for more than fifty years one of the great figures of the English-language theatre.

Dame Judith, who forbids public mention of her age, announces that she was born just before the Boer War and has always had black cats called Buller after the famous Boer leader. The youngest of four children, Dame Judith says she gave her first "great performance" a few seconds after her entrance into the world when she stopped breathing. Today, more than eight decades later, she is a tiny, elegantly dressed figure with reddish hair and very strong features. She uses her hands with practised skill to make a point or to accent her voice, a voice devoid of any type of affectation which can cut through a crowded room without any visible effort in the fragile frame from which it issues.

Dame Judith Anderson, Santa Barbara, 1984

On the day I talked to her, she had spent the weekend staying with a friend at the campus of the local branch of the University of California, where a sixteen-hour weekend marathon of the television serial "I Claudius" was screened for aficionados. She described the performance of Derek Jacobi as the most enthralling she had ever seen, displacing Olivier's Othello which, until that weekend, had been her favourite. The tragedy of age, she said, was that she knew she would never be able to work with Jacobi.

Dame Judith was born in Angus Street, Adelaide. Her parents separated when she was five and she never saw her father again. Both parents died on the opening nights of plays: her father on the night she was opening *Family Portrait* in 1939 (a play in which she portrayed the mother of Jesus), and her mother on the opening night of Robinson Jeffers's *The Tower Beyond Tragedy* in 1951.

At the age of eight, she was winning medals for elocution at temperance meetings, reciting Shakespeare and singing Lieder in the Adelaide Town Hall. At eleven, she was already in greasepaint, acting in various amateur theatrical companies. She calls herself a "born show-off", and once threw a tantrum during a performance because an adult actor, whom she imagined she was desperately in love with, announced that his fiancée was in the audience. She has forgotten his name but, with female doggedness, remembers to this day the name of her unfortunate rival.

She attended school, "as little as possible ... wagging it as often as I could". This may explain her lifelong love affair with the poetry of Shakespeare as she was not at school long enough to have it destroyed, as it so often is by knuckle-cracking Australian chalkies. While others of her age were reluctantly memorising lines from *Hamlet* or *Macbeth*, she was reciting them to win the Diamond Medal for Elocution of the Combined Temperance Societies in Ballarat.

Her father's abrupt departure from the family home followed his unsuccessful investment of £30,000, the family's remaining capital, on a horse at the Adelaide races. Mr Anderson, called "The Silver King", had once owned a number of silver-mines but had gambled them away. With his departure, the family finances worsened, and her mother opened a grocery shop with Dame Judith making the deliveries. In 1914, she suspects that a Sydney uncle, an MLA, assisted the family in moving to Sydney so that Dame Judith could pursue a career in the theatre.

In Sydney, Mrs Anderson opened a boarding house in Macleay Street — "Long gone; I looked last time I was in Sydney" — and Dame Judith, still called Frances Anderson (her baptismal name was

Frances Margaret) forced her way into the theatrical company of the Scottish actor-manager Julius Knight by demanding, at the age of seventeen, an audition for the role of the Empress Josephine in *The Royal Divorce*. She didn't get the role, which she now admits she was not suited for, but impressed Mr Knight sufficiently to be awarded the part of the ingenue. Prior to this, she had made a momentary appearance as a page in James Bentley's *Hamlet*, which ended in total disaster when a malicious cue propelled her onto the stage to parade her tights-encased legs (of which Dame Judith was quite proud) in the middle of Hamlet's "To be or not to be" soliloquy. Mr Bentley was stricken in full flight and by the time he composed himself and finished his speech, Dame Judith had cleared her dressing-room and left.

Dame Judith quickly established herself as a supporting player in Knight's company, and he taught her "everything I know". Pressed as to whether this is hyperbole, she retreats a little. Nobody can teach an actor how to portray character. That inner ability exists or does not exist. But Knight taught her how to move, use her hands, project her voice, walk with a train and all the other techniques of stagecraft actors must first master in order to develop whatever real talent they may have. Years later, she travelled from London to Glasgow to visit him in retirement and thank him for his early encouragement.

In 1918, Dame Judith toured New Zealand with a visiting American company. The American principals admired her work and advised her to try her luck overseas. They warned her that if she remained in Australia she was destined for ever to play second fiddle to imported stars. "Go to God's country", she was advised. She cabled her mother in Sydney to sell up and pack their bags. They were indeed off to "God's country". Dame Judith says she chose America instead of England because she didn't want to add to the wartime congestion. What she does not say, but which seems likely from the personal letters in her papers, is that several of the young men she knew in Australia had been slaughtered at Gallipoli or in France and that wartime London was too painfully close to that wretched carnage. One beau died in the same English hospital bed her brother had occupied for nine months.

Arriving in Los Angeles by steamer, Judith was granted an interview by Cecil B. De Mille as a result of a letter from one of the Tait brothers. She was, De Mille told her, totally unsuitable. Her face was not glamorous, her clothes were wrong, she was just not Hollywood. Later, De Mille was to write and graciously admit how wrong he had been. Rejected by Hollywood, Judith and her mother

spent their last $100 on train tickets to New York.

Arriving in New York without funds, they took a single room in a doctor's house, mother and daughter being forced to share the same bed. Mrs Anderson took in sewing to support them while Dame Judith started a round of "go sees" to the various theatrical agencies. Shortly after they arrived in New York, the "killer 'flu" epidemic of 1918 arrived back with the troops from Europe like a medieval plague, causing thousands of deaths. Dame Judith and her mother caught it and, while both survived, it left them weak for months afterwards.

Still recuperating, Dame Judith got her first job in New York through a sheer fluke. After calling on one theatrical agency on 39th Street unsuccessfully, she felt too tired to catch a streetcar home and decided to rest in the waiting-room of Paul Scott's just across the road, an agency she had not intended visiting. Walking in at exactly the right moment, she was engaged, at $40 a week, to play the second lead in *Rebecca of Sunnybrook Farm* at the 14th Street Stock Company, where the presiding star was the famous Emma Bunting.

They liked her work at the Stock Company and she remained with it for more than a year. With this company, she was in a different play every week. The cast would rehearse a new play by day and perform the current one at night. Dame Judith remembers this as crucial experience. "The director could not help you much, you were on your own; you swam or you sank."

William Gillette, a leading actor-playwright of the period, came to see her one night. He liked her work and cast her in *Dear Brutus* in which she toured throughout 1920. Other productions followed. In 1923, she was advised by the producer of *Peter Weston* to drop the name Frances. Judith, the name she chose, was taken from a character in Shaw's play *The Devil's Disciple*.

Although she had played leads in the Stock Company and later in touring productions, it wasn't Broadway. Her big break came in 1924 in *Cobra* by A. A. Milne. The star in the out-of-town try-out had to be replaced. Dame Judith would get the part for the Broadway opening, provided she could dress herself for it. She couldn't find a gown slinky enough for the second act, but an Australian friend brought her a dress borrowed from the movie actress Dagmar Godowski, whom Dame Judith described as, "big, blousy, fat and beautiful". Wrapping the voluminous garment almost twice around her petite but curvacious body, Dame Judith slunk successfully. The

The acclaimed actress, 1950s (News Ltd)

play was her first Broadway hit.

After *Cobra*, she was rarely out of work. Making decent money at last, she and her mother were able to take separate apartments, just across the hall from each other in a handsome building facing Central Park. She was becoming a very popular actress, and there were several men in her life. One of them may have been, she now believes, the only man she ever really loved. They were together for two years. They separated because she thought he was showing signs of drinking too much. No doubt the memory of her father, whom she says was a heavy drinker, scared her off. She married twice, but both times the marriage failed, the second after just a few days. "I made two rotten choices and that was that."

In 1927, Judith toured Australia in *Cobra*, her first hit, and also played *The Green Man*. The 1930s saw a procession of successes. They included *Strange Interlude* by Eugene O'Neill, *As You Desire Me* by Pirandello, *Behold the Bridegroom*, and of course the celebrated role of Lavinia Mannon in O'Neill's *Mourning Becomes Electra*. In 1934, she toured seventy-nine cities in thirty-one States co-starring with Helen Menkin in the Pulitzer Prize-winning play *The Old Maid* by Zoe Atkins.

Dame Judith is also proud of a couple of her flops. One of them, *Come of Age* by Clemence Dane (the story of the poet Chatterton), she thinks deserved better. Produced as a play but with a full orchestra and choral backing, it won selective approval but was too avant-garde for conventional Broadway audiences and closed after four weeks. In 1936, in America and later in London, she successfully played Queen Gertrude in John Gielgud's *Hamlet*. In 1937–38, she played Lady Macbeth against Laurence Olivier at the Old Vic in London and against Maurice Evans in New York.

Before playing Lady Macbeth, a role she was to play many times (and, in the opinion of many critics, she played it better than any of her peers), she was concerned that the pivotal sleepwalking scene should be totally authentic. She asked a friend who was a doctor at Bellevue Mental Hospital if she could watch a patient actually sleepwalking. A patient was hypnotised before going to bed and duly walked in her sleep for Dame Judith. Dame Judith noticed that the woman talked from the back of her throat and was unsteady on her feet, and she adopted the mannerisms for her own portrayal.

In 1939, there was another controversial flop. It failed in large part because of a boycott by the Catholic Church. The play, *Family Portrait*, was based on an Anatole France story about the family of Jesus. Dame Judith played the Mother, a role that was not in

Playing the title role in *Medea*, Australian tour, 1955 (News Ltd)

accordance with Catholic doctrine on the Virgin Mary. Dame Judith resisted pressure by many leading Catholics in New York to give up the part. In retrospect, she says that perhaps the script did not do justice to France's story. But despite its petty vulgarities, it was "nearly a great play". It was apparently more than "nearly" a great performance. Richard Watts Jr, drama critic of the New York *Herald Tribune* wrote:

"... It would be impossible to imagine the role of the Mother much more beautifully played. Miss Anderson has had a distinguished career in the theatre, but never, I feel sure, has she been so knowing and compassionate and deeply understanding. It is a portrayal of genuine spiritual beauty and fine dramatic authority, and it demonstrates with considerable conclusiveness that Miss Anderson is one of our finest actresses ..."

During the war years, there were more plays and, after her success in *Rebecca* as Mrs Danvers, in 1940, an increasing number of specialised movie roles. In 1941, she did *Macbeth* on stage, again with Maurice Evans and in 1942, the Chekhov play, *Three Sisters*. Before filming *Rebecca* in 1940, she moved her home from New York to Pacific Palisades, a suburb of Los Angeles on the ocean front, where Ronald Reagan lived before his election to the presidency.

Part of the war was spent entertaining troops in the Pacific for the United States Army, first in Hawaii and later in New Guinea. For the first tour, she did *Macbeth*, again playing opposite her old standby Maurice Evans. A story is told by a backstage member of the USO company that presented *Macbeth* in Hawaii. The troops, fresh from some bloody battlefield in the Pacific, came to the concert expecting a burlesque show. As Macbeth and Lady Macbeth were smoothly consummating their love scene midway through the first act, bedlam broke loose in the audience. Cries of "Turn out the lights", "Take it off" and whistles broke out. The director, Private George Schafer (who later produced the "Hallmark Hall Of Fame" television specials), was instructed to bring down the curtain but before he could do so, Dame Judith took over. John Dryer, then a stagehand on the show and now a reporter in California, described what happened:

"Judith Anderson was leaning over Maurice Evans during their love scene, virtually frozen, hoping (I suppose) that the pandemonium would subside. It didn't. She had been half-holding him [but now dropped him] like a sack of wet cement and strode majestically to the footlights to the amazement of everyone. Then, after several long seconds of Miss Anderson's cold stare, came an extemporaneous soliloquy of her own. 'Gentlemen,' she said coolly, 'I do not know how many of you have ever seen a real live play before, but if you'll give us an opportunity, you might be pleasantly surprised. However, if you do not care to give us the common courtesy of your undivided attention, we shall simply close the curtain and I shall go back to my comfortable home in California. I do not *have* to be here, you know ...' Miss Anderson did an about-face and returned to her love scene ... Not only was there nary another outburst from the unruly GIs, but the play finished to a standing ovation."

Dame Judith played *Macbeth* in New Guinea in 1943 and insisted on giving a special performance for Australian troops. The Diggers responded by contributing their own rations to a party in her honour. On a second tour, she dispensed with Shakespeare and the ubi-

---

Playing the nurse in *Medea*, with Zoe Caldwell in the title role, Broadway, 1981 (News Ltd)

quitous Mr Evans and, accompanied by a musical trio, performed recitations and songs on her own.

In 1944, she asked the poet Robinson Jeffers to write her a new, free adaptation of the Euripidean tragedy *Medea*. Jeffers was regarded as the leading contemporary poet of modern Greek tragedy. He promptly agreed and the verse drama was published in 1946 with a dedication to Judith Anderson.

When *Medea* opened in New York in 1947, with John Gielgud playing Jason opposite Dame Judith's Medea, a classic was added to the repertoire of the English-speaking theatre. Brooks Atkinson, the critic of the *New York Times*, whose frown was usually sufficient cause for a Broadway producer to file for bankruptcy, positively beamed at Dame Judith's performance in this play.

"An inspired performance ... superb acting. Her simple-hearted mother of men, full of wonder, pride and misgivings, is played with deep compassion."

For more than thirty-five years, *Medea* was regarded as Dame Judith Anderson's personal property. It was toured nationally and internationally and was produced in Australia in 1955. There was also a television performance for which Dame Judith won an Emmy.

Medea was not to be Dame Judith's last association with Robinson Jeffers. In 1951, she played Electra in Jeffers's *The Tower Beyond Tragedy*. She serves to this day as a Trustee of the Robinson Jeffers Foundation at Carmel, California, which operates a museum and is custodian of Jeffers's papers and literary rights.

In the two decades following the Second World War, Dame Judith was extremely busy. As well as stage work and movies, there were several major television appearances. These included (apart from *Medea*): *The Bridge of San Luis Rey* by Thornton Wilder, *Macbeth*, and *The Cradle Song*, which she did in 1956 for NBC. In 1960, she returned to the Old Vic to do Chekhov's *The Seagull*. She moved from the Los Angeles area to Santa Barbara in 1950 shortly before the death of her mother, whose ungrudging sacrifice and support Dame Judith misses to this day.

It is difficult to get Dame Judith to talk much about Hollywood. She does not regard movies as her medium. Her passion is for the proscenium arch and a warm, responsive audience. Although she appeared in over twenty movies, including several very successful ones (*Rebecca, King's Row, Laura, Cat on a Hot Tin Roof*, for example) she never really enjoyed working to a cold camera. She will say that she enjoyed Hitchcock's *Rebecca* and her role as Mrs Danvers; "For once, everything came together at the right time". Ephraim Katz, in his *The Film Encyclopaedia*, points out that Dame Judith was usually typecast "in unsympathetic and at times sinister roles".

The busy portion of her career ended in the mid-1960s, fifty years after she appeared in *The Royal Divorce* in Sydney in 1915. However, one major role still awaited her. She had always wanted to play Hamlet. Bernhardt had played it as had many other actresses. "The Prince has so many glorious lines", as Dame Judith puts it, and she wanted to do them her way. She had her own views about Hamlet's character which she wanted a chance to portray. She interprets some of his lines as indicating a homosexual guilt. She also had her own ideas on how best to dress Hamlet and the way he should be lit — from the waist up.

In the end, the production that eventuated in 1971 was in no way what she had planned. There was friction between herself and the director William Bell, who dressed the diminutive Dame Judith in huge thigh-boots and built a set consisting of a series of high steps that she was forever climbing and descending. It was a disaster, and many of Dame Judith's friends have asked her why she attempted it. Some have asked in print and since become ex-friends.

While admitting her production failed, Dame Judith remains unrepentant. She quotes a letter from a young girl asking whether the skull used on stage was real or plastic, and remembers a visit backstage from a young couple who complained that they could not hear the clashing of the swords: "There was no skull of course, and there were no swords. What we did was make them think that there was a skull and that what we held in our hands were swords."

In 1981, Dame Judith emerged from semi-retirement to play the nurse in *Medea* on Broadway. As well as playing the nurse on stage, she also played the role of midwife to the production off-stage. As one of the guardians of the Jeffers's Foundation, she thought that something should be done with *Medea*, to keep it alive and to produce royalties for the foundation.

Dame Judith had seen Zoe Caldwell play Sarah Bernhardt and immediately realised that Caldwell was the only actress who could play Medea. She arranged for the foundation to telephone Robert Whitehead who had produced, but not directed, the first *Medea* in 1947. Whitehead is also Zoe Caldwell's husband. (To complete this circle, Zoe Caldwell made her debut in the Australian Elizabethan Theatre Trust production of *Medea* in 1955, in which Dame Judith starred.)

Dame Judith, with the aplomb of a William Morris agent putting together a package, proposed to the Jeffers's Foundation that Whitehead should direct a new *Medea* with Caldwell playing the title-role and Dame Judith the nurse. The Whiteheads were at first aghast at the suggestion, particularly at the idea of Dame Judith, the previous Medea, scuttling around on stage as the nurse. No doubt Robert Whitehead recalled the 1947 observation by Brooks Atkinson:

"It would be useless now for anybody else to attempt the part. Using a new text by Robinson Jeffers, she has set a landmark in the theatre."

There was also the problem of Dame Judith's previous disagreements with Whitehead. The reasons for these remain shrouded in the mists of time, but when Robert Whitehead and Zoe Caldwell called on Dame Judith in Santa Barbara, artistic and historical differences were swept away in a happy cloud of vodka.

The new Whitehead-directed production received mixed reviews, but some were excellent. Zoe Caldwell won a third Tony award for her performance. And Dame Judith received superlative praise for her portrayal of the nurse.

Dame Judith's three working visits to Australia were, in a professional sense, disappointing. The 1927 tour with her first hit *Cobra* was not well received and Dame Judith, with her usual honesty, does not blame the Australian audience. It was not a great play, she says, although it worked well on Broadway. The other play on that tour, *The Green Man*, was better but it was far from being the best of her parts. The Australian production of *Medea* in 1955 was not good; many thought this was primarily due to the poor direction by Hugh Hunt. Zoe Caldwell commented that the only member of the cast who really knew what she was meant to be doing was Dame Judith, and she achieved this by ignoring the director. Finally, there was her last visit to Australia in 1974 to take part in the film *Inn of the Damned* in which an agreement not to change the script was not kept.

When I asked Dame Judith what she would have liked to have done in Australia, she said she thought Australia should have seen a better *Medea* with a proper director and a good supporting cast, and that she would have liked to have played Lady Macbeth in a good company.

Dame Judith was not quite twenty-one when she left Australia in 1918. She has never thought of returning there to live because her roots have long since withered. She doubts whether she will visit her homeland again. She has, however, maintained her Australian citizenship for more than sixty years, an indication of her feelings for her country.

When asked about her great moments, she surprisingly does not mention any of the "biggies". The performances she enjoyed most were the ones she gave to the troops in New Guinea, which could hardly have been, in artistic terms anyway, among her best. The happiest moment of her life was the night the Australian Ambassador rang her from Washington to tell her she would be made a Dame of the British Empire in the 1960 New Year Honours. When she went to London to be invested, the Queen looked at her with some surprise and said, "Did you come all the way to London just for this?"

In March 1982 in the Eisenhower Auditorium of the Kennedy Center in Washington, the curtain rose on the last Washington performance of *Medea*. As usual the rising curtain revealed the silent, motionless figure of the nurse. Spontaneously the auditorium broke into a prolonged standing ovation that lasted for many minutes. The nurse remained silent. Not a flicker of emotion or recognition registered on her face as the applause thundered around her, seemingly without end. The audience was saying a respectful farewell to a grand old trouper. And that grand old trouper was determined not to spoil the new Medea's entrance. The torch had been passed.

In June 1984 the New York theatrical world recognised Dame Judith's contribution to the American stage by renaming the Lion Theatre in her honour. She was almost too busy to attend the dedication ceremony, for Hollywood had once more called on her special skills and she had a featured part in the new *Star Trek* movie. She also has a continuing part as a matriarch in a new soap opera, "Santa Barbara" — a role she continues to play in real life.

JAMES WOLFENSOHN

Not many Australians who have ventured abroad have made their name in banking and finance. It is an area in which Australians have usually not shown great flair or personal initiative. This may be because their domestic banking and finance industries have been highly derivative, or because they have been heavily protected and regulated by paternalistic governments of all colours. James David Wolfensohn is one of the few Australians to have broken that mould.

James Wolfensohn's father Bill was a first-generation Englishman who moved to Australia. James Wolfensohn is a first-generation Australian who has moved to America. When the First World War started, Bill Wolfensohn was studying medicine at St Thomas's Hospital in London, and simultaneously reading law. His studies were never completed. He finished the war as a captain in the Royal Fusiliers, having played an active part in the recruiting of the Jewish Regiment in Palestine.

After the war, he became absorbed in Zionist causes and for a while was secretary to James de Rothschild, working on Jewish matters. Finally, deciding he had little future in England, he and his Belgian-born wife Dora migrated to Australia.

Bill Wolfensohn arrived in Australia just before the Great Depression and bought a brewery at Lithgow in New South Wales. However, he lost his brewmaster during the Depression and was unable to replace him. He ended up losing the brewery as well, and most of his money.

He then opened a small advertising business and consulting firm, advising people how to run businesses. His real passion, however, was the resettlement of European Jews in Australia. He worked endlessly at this, naturally without financial reward.

His wife Dora, from whom James Wolfensohn no doubt inherits his musical talents, was an excellent singer and had a regular session on ABC Radio. She was also an accomplished painter. During the Second World War, Dora operated the Anzac buffet in Hyde Park — this was while working at the Ministry of Munitions — and was later President of the National Council of Jewish Women. Wolfensohn says, in the shorthand of his trade, that neither of them had any "resources" but gave all their time and energy to the Sydney Jewish community.

James Wolfensohn, 1982 (ACP)

Bill and Dora Wolfensohn both died in the 1970s. The only remaining Wolfensohns now in Australia are James Wolfensohn's sister, Betty Raghavan, born ten years before him, who is a Sydney cancer specialist, and Betty's son.

Wolfensohn was born in 1933 in Potts Point, Sydney. The first school he attended was a Catholic school. He clearly remembers winning the annual prize for religious studies. The runner-up, a girl, was also Jewish. From there he moved to the opportunity class at Woollahra Public School which prepared boys for Sydney High School. In the five years he spent at high school, his career almost petered out a couple of times as he sunk towards the bottom of the class. In the end, the Leaving Certificate marks that he managed to achieve were the bare minimum necessary to scrape into Sydney University.

Wolfensohn's first year of a combined arts-law course at Sydney University was almost a wipe-out. He passed one subject out of four. He was only fifteen when he entered university and very immature. He lost himself in the absorption of endless games of chess. He was persuaded to stay at university by a family friend, Julius Stone, the distinguished Professor of International Law, who persuaded him it was not too late to mend his ways. He got through the rest of his university course without incident. He has since been told that years later, the then Vice-Chancellor, when asked whether he remembered Wolfensohn as an undergraduate, described him as the laziest person ever to get through university. There were a few solidifying experiences for Wolfensohn at Sydney University. One was the study of logic at which he excelled. The other was the study of music theory where he was placed second in his class.

In his final years at law school, Julius Stone arranged for Wolfensohn to become an articled clerk with the Sydney law firm of Allen Allen and Hemsley. This firm, together with a few others of equally venerable lineage and reputation, constitute the senior legal firms in Sydney. In the days of which we are now talking, the mid-1950s, they were much smaller than they are today, and State law restricted the number of partners in a legal partnership much more tightly than it now does.

Wolfensohn believes he was the first Jewish articled clerk employed by Allens'.

"In those days, anti-Semitism was not a big thing in terms of

---

President, J. Henry Schroder Bank Trust, New York, 1974 (ACP)

being virulent or obvious, but quite a lot of doors had just not been opened. I had a fairly orthodox religious upbringing, I had gone regularly to synagogue every week and so on, though that became less frequent when I went to university. But I kept the Sabbath and I kept the dietary laws. To this day I keep the dietary laws. The first day of articles, I was totally overwhelmed at the thought of being in Allen Allen and Hemsley; to me it was the pinnacle of legal standing and recognition in the community. And that first day I am taken to lunch in the partners' room. I am sitting there surrounded by senior partners . . . and a waiter puts a plate of pork in front of me. I knew it was then or never so I said: 'I don't eat pork. I'm Jewish and you had better get ready for it.' They did. Allens' were marvellous. They were absolutely pivotal in my life. I made lifelong friends there."

At Allens', Wolfensohn worked closely with a senior partner, G. S. Reichenbach, working in his room as was the custom in those days. Wolfensohn worked at Allens' for three years as an articled clerk and then as an employed solicitor. While at Allens' as an articled law clerk, he was theoretically supposed to be attending law school in the late afternoons, but Wolfensohn rarely went to lectures, working instead in the Allens' library, where he would study for four weeks each year before the exams.

He had taken up fencing at university and he kept it up after becoming a national fencing champion, and in 1956 competed in the Olympics in Melbourne. He had also joined the University Air Squadron, which was of great assistance to him when he was making his arrangements to travel to Harvard.

His interest in Harvard arose as a result of a case he was working on at Allens'. It was a $300 million treble damages claim known as the RCA-Zenith antitrust suit. Allens' were solicitors for RCA, and G. S. Reichenbach, Wolfensohn's senior, being ill, it fell to him, a newly qualified solicitor, to brief the American lawyer that RCA had flown out for this important case. On the second day of the trial, the American passed Wolfensohn a balance sheet and asked him what the net worth involved was. It quickly became apparent Wolfensohn did not know one side of a balance sheet from the other. The American lawyer angrily asked him why he did not go to Harvard and find out.

That night, in the Hotel Rex in Canberra, Wolfensohn wrote to the Harvard Business School for an application. Seven months later, he was actually on his way. Articled clerks do not make enough money to finance trips to America; Wolfensohn arranged transport by talking the affable Fred Osborne, Minister for Air, into arranging a lift for him on an RAAF aircraft. The justification Wolfensohn gave for this was that it would be advantageous for the Air Force Reserve to have on its books an officer who had attended the illustrious Harvard Business School. Osborne hooted with derision but organised it anyway. He was finally flown to America via London on a Hastings owned by the New Zealand Air Force.

In 1957, when Wolfensohn arrived in Harvard, the cost of the two-year course was $7000. Incoming students were advised that they must have $3500 and that they would then be eligible for an advance in aid of $3500. There were no scholarships. Wolfensohn turned up with $270 in his pocket. He quickly made his way to the office of the woman who ran the financial aid programme, Florence Glynn.

Glynn allowed Wolfensohn to start drawing against his advance in his first instead of his second year. Between his first and second years, he made some money working for Angus Lightfoot Walker at Rheem, whom he had met in Australia. In his second year at Harvard, he ran the laundry service. He has since established a scholarship in Australia for Australians who wish to attend the Business School.

Wolfensohn spent two years at Harvard and did indeed get to understand both sides of a balance sheet. He also spent time studying antitrust law at the Harvard Law School and was invited to stay and do a doctorate. He decided instead to spend a year in Europe at the Harvard Institute in Lausanne, near Geneva. This was called the IMEDE Management Development Institute, and was jointly run by Harvard and the Swiss Nestlé Company, for middle-management executives.

In 1957, Wolfensohn met Elaine Botwinick at a rehearsal concert of the Boston Symphony Orchestra. She was a French scholar at nearby Wellesley. They had attended the rehearsals for the same reason — they were free. He and Elaine married in 1961.

When he returned from his year in Europe, Wolfensohn took a job with Rheem International. He became Director of Growth and Development.

"This meant essentially that I went out and looked at every crazy project there was around the world. If it was halfway sensible, somebody more senior would go and take a look at it. It was tremendous experience. I negotiated deals in Nigeria, Greece and India and started to get a sense of international business ... I worked for a chap called Mario Capelli who again was a significant influence on my life. He did what was necessary for all Harvard Business

School people, which was to knock you off your pedestal, bring you down quick, so that you could forget that you'd been educated and get in and learn the business."

After eighteen months, and just married to Elaine, James Wolfensohn decided to return to Australia. While at Harvard, he had established a tiny firm with a few chums from England, Hong Kong and America. He decided now to activate it. His first venture was reasonably successful, the publication of a book on export marketing, financed by the Commonwealth government. His second was a disaster, a $12,000 investment in a small engineering firm in which he was defrauded.

Almost broke, with a young wife on his hands, Wolfensohn decided the life of an undercapitalised entrepreneur had no future, so he surrendered to the blandishments of the Sydney brokerage house of Ord and Minnett. Ord's were in the process of forming Darling and Co., and one of their principals, Michael Gleeson-White, had been advertising for a Harvard MBA or equivalent. Wolfensohn's father, Bill, had written to Gleeson-White telling him there was no such thing as an equivalent to a Harvard MBA and his son, who had one, would soon be available and to please hold on.

Wolfensohn joined Ord's and shortly afterwards was appointed managing director of Darling and Co., the new merchant bank formed by Ord's with Schroder Wagg of London, Jardine Matheson of Hong Kong, and what was then called the Bank of New South Wales.

He was to spend six fruitful years with Darling's. He introduced to it many clients of the standing of BP, Exxon, Grace, and Continental Oil. He established a team of people of whom he was extremely proud. Several of his former assistants at Darling's have now become significant figures in their own right.

Wolfensohn and Gleeson-White, while at Darling's, developed the first intercompany deposit market. This involved finding a way of enabling the market to function without attracting State transfer taxes which were levied on all documentation. Wolfensohn set up an ingenious system of company IOUs that were recorded in the accounts of a company but not handed on to another company. Darling's, under Wolfensohn, also pushed the concept of convertible notes as a reputable form of security.

Wolfensohn did a lot of early work persuading overseas investors that Australia was a respectable place to invest in mineral developments. It might seem hard to believe today, but traditionally Australia was not a place for serious as opposed to promotional

Partner, Salomon Brothers, New York, 1977 (ACP)

mineral investment. Wolfensohn did a great deal of work in persuading overseas firms that Australia's future was in natural resources. He did the first financings for Alcoa of its project in Western Australia and also handled the first Savage River financing in Tasmania.

The top chair of corporate finance at Darling's was not going to keep a cosmopolitan like James Wolfensohn in Sydney for ever. This is how Wolfensohn saw the situation:

"In those days, which were pre-jet, everything took longer; communications were not instantaneous, there was no direct dialling. An overseas trip was a big thing. An overseas call was still an overseas call. Australia was a more parochial place. Happy, rich, still agriculturally based, with few social tensions and good weather. But it was scarcely international. You could name on the fingers of both hands the recognisable Australians in finance and industry around the world."

By the middle 1960s, James Wolfensohn was ready to leave Australia. His work was becoming more international and he was too far from the centre of things. His wife, a native New Yorker, was about as far from New York as you can get. As well he became involved in a bitter company acquisition in which his colleague John Broinowski was involved on the other side. He felt it time to leave and mentioned this to Gordon Richardson, then Chairman of Schroder's in London (and later head of the Bank of England), and also to Sigmund Warburg, of the London banking house of the same name. Both offered Wolfensohn jobs. Wolfensohn accepted a directorship of J. Henry Schroder Wagg, the London merchant bank.

"It mightn't sound so big a jump now. In those days it was a tremendous act of faith on his part really ... I went over there and found myself in a wholly English environment, under the protection of Gordon Richardson. In effect, Gordon created a job for me, helping to set up the international operations of the Schroder Wagg group."

There was some hostility to Wolfensohn from the start. The idea of any banking or financial expertise coming from Australia or anywhere outside the British Isles was anathema to these people. One of the founders of Schroder Wagg, Alfred Wagg, was Jewish, so although Wolfensohn was at that time the only Jew on the staff, he considered the odd examples of anti-Semitism he encountered to be random and not the real source of the hostility which was directed towards him. His "colonialism" was the explanation.

Wolfensohn, however, always had the confidence of Gordon Richardson, the top man, and because his work was largely international, it was to him he reported. Wolfensohn and his wife, Elaine, enjoyed swinging London. It was the end of the 1960s and London was enjoying a burst of real prosperity. The Wolfensohns had a lovely house and their third child, Adam, was born in Britain, their daughters Sara and Naomi having been born in Sydney.

Wolfensohn found that his experience in Sydney with Darling's had been unique and invaluable. He had made contacts most people at his level in England or America could not possibly have done. This was partly due to the pioneering status of Darling's when it started. It was the only merchant bank in Sydney for some time, with the man running it a graduate of the Harvard Business School, which made him a friendly face in a foreign jungle. Americans have their own way of doing business and an MBA from Harvard indicates that those ways will be clearly understood and appreciated at that address.

These old connections added to the resentment that Wolfensohn encountered in Schroder's London headquarters. At his age and level of seniority, he was not expected to know this sort of person. It screwed up all sorts of office traditions and pecking orders. The English factory worker is constantly attacked for his poor output and his restrictive work practices. It should never be supposed his bowler-hatted superiors conduct their affairs any more efficiently.

Wolfensohn's work took him away from England more and more. He was selling the virtues of the international financial market — the Eurodollar market and the Eurobond market — which was just beginning to develop.

"In those days you didn't have facsimile transmission, and you didn't have satellite communications, so that if you came from London to Milwaukee or Pittsburgh or San Francisco, and you were a merchant banker, you were bringing news from the battlefield much as N. M. Rothschild brought news of the Battle of Waterloo. I also started to go to the Far East; to Japan, to Hong Kong, to Singapore."

At the beginning of 1970, Gordon Richardson took a second risk with Wolfensohn. Schroder's operated a 600-man commercial bank in New York and they needed a new chief executive for it. After various American dignitaries were considered, Wolfensohn got the job, at thirty-seven. The bank was the J. Henry Schroder Bank Trust Company and there were also two associated companies, the Schroder Trust Company and Schroder Rockefeller, that Wolfensohn was expected to run. Elaine was ecstatic to be back in Manhattan. Wolfensohn was excited, despite his complete lack of experience in the commercial banking world.

Wolfensohn said it was a courageous move of Richardson's to dump an Australian Jew into the heartland of American Waspdom. The bank he had become President of was a well-respected member of the "club". It had a long history of international banking and foreign exchange, and "superlative" relationships with the great American banks, but in the field of commercial banking it had failed to distinguish itself.

For Jimmy and Elaine Wolfensohn it was an exciting way to arrive in town. After several years as one of thirty directors of Schroder's, here he was in New York as President of a prestigious bank. With the job went a chauffeur-driven Cadillac and a Park Avenue apartment.

"We always seemed to manage to spend everything we made but we lived pretty well — and Elaine had a little money which we always had there, knowing it was a nest-egg. We both had a lust for life and for doing things. We also thought it was the right thing to do for the business, although I think that was a rationalisation more than a real motive, but it launched me into the middle of the New York financial scene with a neutral platform. You were everybody's friend as President of Schroder's."

The next five years passed in a whirl of productive activity. Although Schroder's was a commercial bank, it was mainly a wholesale one and concentrated on services not then generally available in all American banks. These included financing international trade, putting syndicate credits together for the Euromarket, and all forms of foreign exchange operations. These activities have become more widely available in recent years. In 1970, the mainstream American banking community by and large still regarded a credit card as a daring new idea. Deregulation has taught them otherwise.

In 1975, Wolfensohn was cruising the Galapagos Islands with Dick Dusseldorp on Dusseldorp's futuristic yacht when he heard on the shortwave radio that gold had dropped $200, that the Deutschmark had been revalued, and that Gordon Richardson had become Governor of the Bank of England. Wolfensohn felt like staying at the Galapagos Islands for ever. All his investment decisions had been turned upside down overnight. His patron and principal supporter at Schroder's had vanished in a puff of gubernatorial smoke in the direction of Threadneedle Street.

He stayed in New York for another year and was then moved back to London with the grand-sounding title of Group Chief Executive and Deputy Chairman of Schroder's. The move to London involved a substantial drop in financial return which Wolfensohn accepted because he had expectations he would become the Chairman of Schroder's. He felt that he had been given enough indication by those that mattered that if he came back he would get the job.

On his return to England, he was given the big corner office and helped the then Chairman, Michael Verey, run the firm; but without an operating division of his own, he quickly lost ground in the battle for the chairmanship that consumed the firm. The directors were split into two camps, those who supported Wolfensohn, and those who wanted a chairman with a traditional English background.

Finally Wolfensohn realised he was not going to win this one and that it was time to head for the fire escape. In the spring of 1977, he moved his family quietly to New York. He worked on in the London office throughout the summer, by which time the family had been installed in New York and the children enrolled in school. Then, in

Partner, Salomon Brothers, New York, 1981 (ACP)

October 1977, he announced he was leaving.

Wolfensohn is reluctant to speak in detail about his last year with Schroder's. He still carries with him a letter from Sir Sigmund Warburg, the distinguished German-born merchant banker, which quotes from his own mother, who said: "There are those who look at such events as disappointments and become poorer, and those who look at them as experiences and become richer."

A number of offers from American investment banks were received, but to the surprise of the street, Wolfensohn joined Salomon Brothers. Salomon Brothers formerly had a rather grey image as a large but traditional American bond-trading house. However, in the early 1970s, under the then leadership of William Salomon and John Gutfreund, the firm had expanded, entering both the international credit and corporate financing markets. As its activities widened, its partners became much richer. One table published in the January 1978 issue of *Institutional Investor* shows the Salomon net worth increased from $34.7 million in 1969 to $191.7 million in 1977. The offer of a partnership in such an asset-laden firm must have been alluring indeed to a man now well into his forties and still without any capital of his own.

Wolfensohn was to stay at Salomons' for five years. The period was obviously mutually beneficial. At the end of that period, Wolfensohn was to leave a rich man and Salomon Brothers was able to point to a reorganised corporate finance department and a number of well-publicised operations that Wolfensohn had conducted for it, particularly the now historic Chrysler bail-out. James Wolfensohn is the corporate heart surgeon who fixed Lee Iacocca with his shiny new transplant. In the years since, the patient has become a fully fledged media celebrity. His "doctor" celebrated his fiftieth birthday by playing the cello at Carnegie Hall.

It was while President of the Schroder bank in New York that Wolfensohn had first managed to link his love of music with his job. He had become a member of the board of Carnegie Hall, and had arranged a concert to open the new lower Manhattan branch of the bank. He turned the bottom floor of the bank into a garden and the 300 guests were treated to a Schubert recital by Vladimir Ashkenazy, followed by a candlelight dinner.

For the more prosaic Salomon Brothers, actively seeking to cut a swathe in the international markets, Wolfensohn arranged a special evening at London's Covent Garden. It was the first time that a chamber ensemble had been performed there. The three musicians were Vladimir Ashkenazy pianist, Itzhak Perlman violinist, and cellist Lynn Harrall. Following the music there was supper for the invited audience of English notables in the Crush Bar. More than one columnist commented at the time Wolfensohn joined Salomons' that they were acquiring a little "class" as well as a top piece of manpower.

In the financial world it was often said the one drawback about a partnership in Salomon Brothers was that it was difficult to get capital withdrawn from the partnership. But Wolfensohn was apparently fortunate in that his departure from the firm coincided with its takeover by a firm that is listed on the New York Stock Exchange. He was able to leave with most of his capital. What remained was invested in a public corporation listed on the Stock Exchange and not a private partnership.

Now in his early fifties, he has arranged his affairs so that he spends as much time engaged in charitable and philanthropic activities as in making money. Wolfensohn has been moving easily among the sleek and mobile private and investment bankers for a quarter of a century. Yet personal wealth came to him quite late and quite quickly. At forty-four he was a talented piece of manpower with a very small net worth. Five years later he was worth several million dollars and working for himself.

His own firm is very much an extension of the Wolfensohn persona. The client list is not large, it comes from all over the world and includes a couple of governments. It occupies prime space, and the finest meals and best cigars are served on the premises. Of his general civic activities, his dynamic leadership of Carnegie Hall has been widely acknowledged in a city not noted for its gracious compliments. He is also President of the Institute of Advanced Studies at Princeton and maintains his interest in Israel as Chairman of the Jerusalem Foundation which serves Jews and Arabs in that city.

A couple of years ago, Wolfensohn took out American citizenship. He did this because he was short-listed for the top job at the World Bank. For this job United States citizenship was essential. In the end the job went to another name on the list — the President of the Bank of America — a defeat perhaps, yet heady stuff for the boy from Sydney High.

GERMAINE GREER

It was on a hot autumn day that Germaine Greer arrived at our house in Santa Barbara. The local sirocco, known as the Santa Ana, was funnelling hot blasts of air at us from the desert to the east and south. My son had picked her up in Los Angeles in a car which was not air-conditioned and they had had a blistering drive up the coast from Los Angeles. She was dressed in a designer track suit — elegant but steamy — and carried an empty champagne bottle which she had swigged on the way up in a futile attempt to keep cool. Now in her forties, she continues to be a strikingly attractive woman. Her hair is longer and she had gained a few kilos since I last saw her almost ten years ago, but she has lost none of her intensity or lanky green-eyed charm.

Greer became a media-event in 1970 when she published *The Female Eunuch* and she has remained one ever since. She is a constant and invigorating television "personality" on both sides of the Atlantic, and since *The Female Eunuch*, has published another book, on women painters. Until recently she was spending five months a year at the University of Tulsa, Oklahoma (where she is Director of the Tulsa Center for the Study of Women's Literature) and the rest of the year in London, where she spent much of her time working on two new books, one on Shakespeare, and the recently released *Sex and Destiny*, a work on human fertility. Human reproduction and fertility, particularly in the Second and Third Worlds, are increasingly her preoccupation today. For several years she has been trying to interest a major television producer in doing a series on this subject. When I last spoke to her, she had just flown to Colombia for five days in connection with this project. For many years she has also maintained a small farm in Tuscany.

I talked to her about her life before she broke silence with *Eunuch*. She was thirty years old when it was released. I wanted to know what lay behind that passionate stream of anger:

"My grandmother was a barmaid in Bendigo. She pulled beer in the family pub which was the Golden Swan and is now the YWCA. She was seduced by an Italian commercial traveller and her first child was born out of wedlock. When she got sick of struggling with this child, her brothers went and found the commercial traveller and forced him to make an honest woman of her. My mother was born

---

Germaine Greer in the March for Women's Equal Pay, Sydney, 1972 (News Ltd)

after that. It's a very classic Australian story in that none of my family made a serious attempt to find out who we were or where we came from. In fact, my grandmother burned all the family records. Unlike other colonials, many Australians just aren't interested.

"My grandmother died about twelve years ago. She was a loving soul — very — and she longed to help us all, even with money, of which she had very little. And in fact, she often did. She would have liked to know a lot more about what I was doing but I never really told her. After a while, she stopped speaking to my grandfather (the Italian commercial traveller). For thirty years she didn't speak to him; brilliant performance! He had a stroke in his car outside the door of the house they still shared, never speaking. She didn't even look in the window of the car, so he sat there in a coma for three days before they found him. When he had a moment of lucidity in the hospital, she still refused to speak to him. 'I haven't talked to him for thirty years, why should I start now?' I don't think that's a very unusual Australian story. No, we're very destructive of our roots. You could never produce a television series like 'Roots' in Australia because nobody gives a shit. It has nothing to do with the convicts. Their descendants would be glad to know their ancestors were convicts. Think of the Macarthurs and the Onslows. They actually do know where they came from but they were so boring. None of us wants to be quite so boring.

"My father, as far as I can make out, was born in Durban, South Africa, and came to Tasmania when he was three. His mother's name was Rachel Weiss, so she was obviously central European Jewish. I suspect that his father was also Jewish. Daddy looks like the Duke of Edinburgh and passed as a gentile all his life, which you could only do in Australia. When I went to England, I asked my father if I could look up his family and he said 'No'. He got me to promise that I wouldn't. Peter Scolthorpe, who comes from Tasmania, says his family knew my father's father in Launceston. I think old Mr Greer went back to England but I can't find out until Daddy's dead. My father was a cadet-major at school, and so as soon as it looked as if Australia was going to war he joined up.

"The RAAF was not involved in hostilities at that stage, so he joined the RAF and went first to Egypt and then to Malta as an intelligence officer. Now frankly speaking, the father I know would never have got into intelligence. But I think he was very smart then. He had an office in the cliffs at Dingli in Malta and he was part of an intelligence operation that was being fed top-secret material from the ultra-machine project. He was getting all kinds of messages about

With Mike Willesee, Sydney, 1973 (News Ltd)

German movements against Allied shipping in the Mediterranean. They were not allowed to warn the Allied ships because it would have given away the fact that German codes were being broken. Eventually, I think my father collapsed under the weight of the knowledge that men on active service were dying and he was living this charmed life in his bunker at Dingli. My guess would be that one day he just began to cry. He was a person with a lot of responsibility — his title was Secret and Confidential Publications Officer — and he never talks about his job because, apart from anything else, they took him to India and debriefed him, rather unpleasantly I surmise.

"When he came back to Australia, he was totally disabled. I remember meeting him at the railway station. He was the last person left on the platform. We'd been up and down, up and down the platform — I was six years old — until there was only this old man left standing there in an RAF greatcoat that grey-blue colour, this skinny little man with an old face and his lower teeth gone. My mother walked up to him and said, 'Rich?'; and he said, 'Peg?'. I'd never seen him at all. And we took him home and he was the head of our family and that was that. The thing that was wonderful, I now realise, is that he just lived a normal life. The only sign of his disablement was that he couldn't deal with any emotional stress. He did his job well as a space salesman for Advertiser Newspapers. Bit of a dead loss from one point of view, but from another he let us lead a freer life than we might otherwise have been able to do. The thing I find so interesting is that he let us imagine we belonged to a high stratum of society. We thought of ourselves as upper middle class.

"I always went to convent schools. I could tell the usual Catholic horror stories but they're not important. I went to St Columbus in Elwood. Then I went to Sacred Heart in Sandringham and then to Holy Redeemer, Ripponlea. From the time I was eleven my education did not cost anybody anything. I had scholarships. The scholarships did not make me think I was different; I was just the person who was best at that sort of thing. I was so bad at sports that it was a pretty good corrective the other way round. We played softball, and one of the reasons I adore baseball today is that I know the rules from softball. I think it is the best game anybody has played in the history of the human race. There were lots of things you were praised for at school but not scholastic ability. They regarded that as a gift from God. They were much more likely to praise you for personality traits.

"When I was fourteen, I wanted to be a nun. By the time I was fifteen, I knew I did not believe in God. If I had really believed in God I would have been a nun. It's the central premise that collapsed. The wanting to be a saint has to do with adolescent passion. You're thinking you're going to love God, you're going to love him hard. I mean to death! He has to have your whole life because anything else in your whole life is not worth giving. I wasn't the only person who was in love with God when I was fourteen. Had to be in love with something. I remember one nun called Sister Raymond who knew that I was an exceptional art student. I also remember another nun who taught me called Sister Eymard, because she was very intelligent. That's unusual amongst nuns. If my Church had any brains, children like me would be taught by Jesuits — not by nuns at all. We require much higher educational levels. The nuns were not smart enough. If I'd been taught by Jesuits I would still be Catholic. The good thing about the nuns is that they taught quietly. I have taught in a State school system and the screaming and shouting is terribly coarsening to children.

"When I was at school, I used to get on my bicycle and ride for hours. I never went out with anybody. One day, I was about sixteen, I rode to a wharf and discovered a man painting. I stood behind him and watched him painting. He was kind of artsy looking. He had a slight hump actually and after a while I said, 'Well the clouds are quite expressive', or something equally grudging. And he turned around and said, 'Oh, you're interested in painting', or something. I said, 'Yes'. And so we had an impassioned conversation, as of two art lovers lost in the great wasteland that was Australia. We walked back down the pier and he said, 'Can I take you out?' He did take me out, to the real live theatre. I went in my mother's high-heeled shoes, a pencil-skirt, bat-winged jacket. On the way home in the tram we had a rather risqué conversation. That struck me as strange. That's been the pattern ever since, the virgin who speaks in risqué fashion. Then when we got home he kissed my hand and I nearly hit him. I realised it was ridiculous. You can't got out with somebody who's ridiculous. He rang up a few times and I said, 'No, I can't ever go out. I've got to get my scholarship' or something like that. In fact, I never had any trouble getting my scholarships. In the matriculation exam I was second in the State for the State Junior Government Scholarship and Anita, the girl who sat next to me, was the first in the State. I couldn't believe Anita was first because I knew I was smarter. Her maths must have been better than mine. But it wasn't a question of thinking I was awfully smart really. I had surprisingly few distractions. I had no pocket-money. I never went out. I loved my schoolwork — and it was fucking easy. I found it much harder to learn the rules of gin rummy than I did to learn the rules of French grammar. I still can't play gin rummy.

"We went to look at Melbourne University during our final year at school. I knew it was waiting for me, and I was waiting for it. I knew it was going to be mine. And I knew I was not going to be in the Newman Society. The tricky thing about going to the university was that I knew I had to get away from home. I had three scholarships: a Senior Government Scholarship, a Diocesan Scholarship and a Teacher's College Scholarship. I was made to give up the other two scholarships and take the Teacher's College Scholarship, which was a craven thing to do because anybody who took the trouble to observe me for five minutes would have known I was never going to teach in the State system. I got a living allowance (this was 1956) of £8 a week. I ran away from home twice. I ran away at the end of my first year at university. They didn't give us any money when we went on summer vacation, the idea being we got the money at the end of the long vacation to buy our books for the new year. We had no money for lodgings or anything like that. So the summer came and I didn't have any money. One afternoon, at home, I opened the fridge, and there were some bananas. I said, 'Can I have a banana?'; my mother said: 'Those bananas are for my children. You can't have anything to eat until you bring home some money for this house.' I'd worked my butt off all year, had a breakdown, been put on sedation but thrown the pills away and done the exams without them. The university environment was such a shock to my system and I had lost my balance. I had gone to uni all winter without a coat sitting on the train from Mentone to Carlton with my teeth chattering. So I thought it can't be any worse if I try and live off my allowance by myself. Living at home was so far away anyway. It was university, then home, and no time for anything else. So when she said the bananas are 'for my children' I said, 'OK, bye-bye'. I had a little briefcase. I put in a nightie, a bottle of Schiaprelli 'Schocking', a hairbrush and a translation of Ovid's *Metamorphoses*. I went to the station and got on the train and started to be happy. I thought this is it. Life begins now. I went and stayed at a house in Hawthorne Road with some guys who were at the university. I rang my father because I thought I should say I'm all right; those things that runaways say. Nobody gave a stuff whether I was all right or not actually. That was the funniest thing. Then I found out from someone that my parents had reported me to the police and I was under age and I was living in a house with three men and I had no income. So I went home rather than ending up in prison, because that would have been unfunny. When I got home, I lay on my bed and my mother came in and said, 'Who let all the flies in?' and I knew I was home. Oh, boy! So I got through the second year somehow or other and then I left home again at the end of that year.

"Then I learnt I could do all sorts of things. I was a waitress lots of times, but the best time was when Goldy (Brian Goldsmith) opened a restaurant in Toorak Road. It was called Goldy's. By that time, I knew a lot of people in television and the media and I ran the backroom for him where all the television people used to come after hours. I found out that I could make a lot of money. I was actually infringing on my teacher's scholarship by working. I was then in the third year of a combined English-French honours course. I wouldn't have done the French, but with the teacher's scholarship you had to take more than one major. By then I was living in a loft at Carlton. I had lots of adventures then. I got raped and beaten up. I had affairs with Goldy and Athol Smith, the fashion photographer. I don't mind if you mention names. I believe in kicking ass and taking names, talking loud and drawing a crowd. The funny thing was my father hated Athol Smith with a passion; because he was so elegant. My father was elegant, too, but in a totally straight and unambiguous

---

Director, Tulsa Center for the Study of Women's Literature, 1979 (News Ltd)

way. When he saw Athol get on a tram in Collins Street with a bunch of violets and a rolled umbrella, exquisitely dressed, he practically threw up. Athol was a very exciting man but he was elusive. I could never work out what to do with him. He was always trying to give me to Gene Barrakat and if there was anybody who really wasn't interested, it was Gene Barrakat.

"I was raped just after leaving home for the second time by a boy who had played football for Xavier; just the sort of boy my mother would have liked me to marry. He was a stranger to me but not to anybody else at the party where it happened. There's a typical Australian way of dealing with things. We were at this party and he kept asking me to come outside and I said: 'Everybody else is kissing right here, why can't we kiss right here?' And he said: 'No, I want you to come outside.' He wanted a light for his cigarette or I wanted a light for mine, who knows. How stupid we were in those days! We went into the kitchen and when we went outside we were on the wrong side of the house. The party was in the back and we were in the front. He said: 'Just come for a walk.' It was too early to start screaming. People never understand these stories. You feel such a fool calling for help before there's any reason to call for help. But I knew I was in trouble.

"We walked down the street and he said, 'Get into this car'. I got into the car. Then he started acting strangely and I tried to get out of the car. Then he got a lot nastier and I got the door shut on my head and few other little choice moves. When I got out of the car, I couldn't walk. I fell on the nature strip and he said, 'What's the matter with you?' I realised he was insane. He didn't realise what damage he'd done. He didn't break any of my teeth or blacken my eyes, but all the insides of my thighs were torn and bruised; then it's a real Australian story because we walked back towards the house and all I could think of was, 'I've got to get home'. All raped women have the same feeling, 'I have to wash myself. I just have to get clean somehow.' I'd fucked a few guys by that time. Sometimes it was a mistake and sometimes it wasn't. But when it was a mistake, it was my mistake. It wasn't forced on me. I really felt as if somebody had made me eat shit. I was certain that anyone who looked at me could tell what had happened to me. They could certainly tell that I was beaten up.

"I remember going into the garage and looking through the garage door into this patio where the party was, and the guys who I'd come to the party with were at the keg and they wouldn't come. So I had to walk the gauntlet. They were too drunk to even notice. 'Please take me home. I've got to go home.' Anyway they didn't take me home. They said, 'Yes, in a minute; go and sit in the car; here are the keys'. They gave me the keys and I sat in the car and after a while I began to throw up. I felt deadly cold and I realised I was in shock and I had to do something. So I went out on the road and flagged a passing motorist. I said, 'I've been raped, I've been beaten up, will you please take me home?' They took me home immediately.

"When the guys came out to the car and found I wasn't there, they realised something was really wrong. They came home and found me on the bed, by this time, practically unconscious. I was living in Brian Goldsmith's flat at this time. Then a couple of weeks later, they did something very interesting. They brought the bloke responsible into the flat and I just nearly fainted. I thought, 'They can't be doing this to me'. But they brought him in and they said to me, 'Is this him?' Apparently he had done this sort of thing before. He did it again too. Then they asked him, 'You like to go to Portsea, don't you?' and he said, 'Why, yes'. They said, 'Don't go there any more because if we see you there we're going to kill you'. They asked him if he went to Buffalo Falls Creek and when he said he did they said, 'Not any more you don't'. So they dealt with it that way, a very Australian way. What's more, the guy believed them. He moved from Melbourne and I didn't see him again until he came into a store I was in and I behaved very strangely and nobody understood why. He's still around and still swears I'm mistaken. Whenever I see this man I go cold, sort of stand there and say, 'That's the man', and he says, 'No, no ... not me ... it's someone else'.

"From Melbourne University I remember Leon Fink, whom I loved with all my heart; Irvin Rockman whom I love with another part of my heart, I guess; Dick Pratt and Peter Sepir and Peter and Nona Teller — all Jews. Then there was Julia Clifton who is now married to a French diplomat in Rome, and there was Ann Knappet who's now Ann Polis, who is involved in the trade union movement. And ... hmmm ... I remember all my teachers. Barry Humphries was not there then. He was a character in the bohemian world with Peter O'Shaughnessey. I think Peter O'Shaughnessey is probably the most disappointing person I have met in my life. I'm stunned we thought he was so important. I helped make several of the exhibits in Barry Humphries's Dada art show, including the custard for 'Puss'n Boots'. I was not paid but I thought it was great fun. I worshipped him anyway. We all did. But the people from the university are not important to me except for Sam Goldberg who taught English. I remember small people and many totally mediocre and dishonest people. John Perceval, very talented but quite destructive; Martin

Boyd, second rate; Mary Boyd, first rate; Clifton Pugh in those days was a very good painter — think of that for a novelty. I belonged to 'the drift' in those days. 'The drift' was not like the Sydney 'push' which was unified intellectually. It was a lifestyle, it represented a way of just hanging around. It was full of shit I'm afraid. I always knew that. I knew it was second rate.

"Before I graduated in '59, I went to Sydney. I had no hostility towards Melbourne but I knew it was second rate. I did not think Sydney was first rate either, but what happened was that two people from Sydney came down and stayed with me in my loft. And when they were going I went to Sydney with them. I found out that in Sydney there were at least intellectually rigorous people and that they could teach me something. At least they could teach me more about the way I already thought. I was already an anarchist. I just didn't know why I was an anarchist. They put me in touch with the basic texts and I found out what the internal logic was about how I felt and thought. They were very funny because at first I wouldn't say 'fuck'. I thought it was very common. They used to tease me about saying 'fuck'.

"Finally, I went back to Melbourne to sit for my exams. I had been in Sydney some weeks and skipped all my classes. I wasn't going to get my degree at all because the Sydney thing was all against getting one's degree. At some stage, I think I must have thought to myself, 'This is silly'. Because the teaching at Melbourne University was the best I was going to get for the rest of my life. I now realise that. I was being taught by the *best*; not my teachers, but the other students. I was a member of a seminar group; there were twenty-one of us. All of us except two casualties have gone on to become university teachers. That's very unusual for one seminar. We were all so sharp, hard-working and very passionate. I had had quite good fun conducting an anti-seminar in opposition to my teachers. It wasn't because I thought my teachers were no good. It was because I thought my teachers were *very* good. It was important to maintain ideas that ran counter to theirs because they had a way of quenching us with rightness. We held these anti-seminars in my loft, which was right opposite the university, and they went on all night. We were very good really. I've never seen a group of students as gifted or as hard-working as we were. I think that the English honours programme offered at Melbourne at that time was as good as that offered at any university in the world. I've taught now in a lot of universities, and I've seen a lot of products from other universities and I think it was amazingly good. It was an unusual . . . concatenation of the students and the teachers. I tried, when I was at Cambridge, to set up a voluntary student group that would go on from where their classes left off. Much too hidebound.

"In the exams my French results were not too good. I got involved in a stupid sexual blackmail situation with someone at the university. I was much too honourable to tell the professor about it; I just cut my classes. And as a result of cutting my classes, and going to Sydney, I didn't do very well in French. The English Department wanted me to stay in Melbourne and teach for them, but the committee that made the appointments assessed my combined English and French results. So I went to Sydney, joined the 'push' and lived with a wharf labourer called Roelof. I lived in North Sydney and hung around all the regular 'push' places. Jim Baker was the resident guru then. After a while, I left Roelof and went to Sydney University to get my MA. Sam Goldberg took over the English Department at Sydney just after I got my MA and I was appointed senior tutor in English. Goldberg told me I had to go to Cambridge to finish my training as a Leavisite, but unfortunately I went to Cambridge to become a Renaissance scholar instead.

"I went to Cambridge as an affiliated student, which enables you to get a BA in two years. I thought the one I had probably wasn't good enough. I was completely wrong. Cambridge offered an inferior version of the same thing. After the first term, I realised they were not going to teach me anything so I transferred to the Ph.D programme. I decided to do my doctoral dissertation on Shakespeare. That was unusual. You're not encouraged to do doctoral dissertations on Shakespeare because it's so hard to write anything new. You are warned that you have little chance of passing if you want to do your doctorate on Shakespeare. I wrote mine about Shakespeare's early comedies, and the reason I was allowed to do so is because when I was in Australia I learnt to speak French and German and Italian almost as well as I spoke English. So I was able to read all the continental Renaissance comedies. The English have always assumed that Shakespeare had continental models. If you really read the continental models you'll find out he didn't. It's much more important to realise how experimental he was. Usually you only know that things are experimental because they fail. Anyway, they gave me my Ph.D, possibly the only doctorate they have given for Shakespeare since the war. I'm not a little proud of it. Among the people who count, other Shakespearean scholars, I'm respected. It's just that I haven't written anything about Shakespeare for a long time. I'm supposed to be doing a book for Oxford University Press on

Shakespeare's thought. But I haven't done that. So poor Henry Hardy at Oxford, who's terribly patient and nice, just waits and waits and waits.

"What's Cambridge like? When I first went there I wanted to be politically active, and socially lively. It's neither of those things. But if you're a scholar to the bone, the way I have become with the passage of time, then six months at Cambridge is like a dream. First of all, it's stunningly beautiful. Secondly, you can find out anything you want to know. If you have a problem, there is always someone in Cambridge who knows something about that problem. Intellectual problems, I mean. I was twenty-five when I came to Cambridge, and I wound up as the great sexual counsellor. I was dreadfully older. English sexuality gave me the heebie-jeebies. Still gives me the heebie-jeebies actually.

"After I left Cambridge, I got a junior lecturer's job at Warwick University. Something like £1100 a year and tax at forty per cent. I couldn't afford a car — no way — and the only way you could ever do anything in the Midlands was to have a car. I lived in a bedsitter owned by a miserable doctor. I was not allowed to bring my own furniture. I didn't belong anywhere. I was miserable. One of the senior people there took an interest in me. Not a very noble or elevated interest. I tried to set him up so I could blackmail him. I arranged to have one of my students catch him in my room. It passed the time. I think he knew what was going on.

"A friend from Cambridge who was working for Granada Television asked me up to Manchester for an audition. I told him I was not interested in doing a comedy series. 'I'm an Australian, I don't belong in this country ...' and so forth. He said to just come up. So I went up there and I ended up doing a television show in Manchester. The university did not seem to mind. They even let me keep the money I got from Granada, which they would not do in America where all outside earnings belong to the university. I don't think they minded as long as I did my job at the university properly, and I was a good teacher. They did mind, however, when I got married in 1968.

"Once I was married, it made me realise the trouble we women can get into. I was just not a free agent any more. Everything I did was criticised. He was really very destructive. Ann Polis sent me some letters I had written years before I wrote *The Female Eunuch* and I

On "The Michael Parkinson Show", Sydney, 1983 (News Ltd)

was saying the same sort of things then that I said in the book in 1969. It was about going to parties and trying to join in conversations and being ignored. The English like to make a great story out of why I am a feminist and say that it is because Australian men are so dreadful. They've got to be kidding. I'd rather fuck an Australian than an Englishman any time. Any time.

"How did the book come about? I had this agent. Agents are responsible for a multitude of sins. I had finished the television show and one day I went to see her. She said, 'Why don't you write a book?' She said that it was the fiftieth anniversary of female suffrage or some such bullshit. 'You should write a book about why female suffrage failed.' I remember losing my temper. I thought, 'What are we talking about! Women didn't get the vote until there was nothing left worth voting for. And what do you think the vote accomplishes anyway?' So I felt really cranky about this. About two days later, I went to lunch with Sonny Mehta, an Indian who was at Cambridge with me and who is a brilliant publisher. He asked me to give him some ideas for books. 'I'm not asking you to lunch to look into your eyes', he said. I gave him a few ideas and told him that my dumb agent had come up with an idea about writing a book about female suffrage. I began to explain how silly the idea was and I flew into a rage. All the best things happen to me when I get cross. I just sort of raged for a while and when I had finished raging, Sonny said, 'That's the book I want. Why don't you come back to the office and we will sign a contract?' I said, 'Sonny you'll never sell it. It will be remaindered.' And he said 'No, no, no!' and we signed a contract. Total advance £750, £250 on signature.

"I showed the first chapters to Sonny and he said nothing. And I knew I hadn't done it. One day, I suddenly realised it had to be written in short chapters; otherwise nobody would read it because women don't have spare time and their concentration span is generally brief. So I began writing short chapters. Sonny read them and gave them back to me speechless as usual. But I could tell by the look in his eyes that I was doing the right thing now. It was only a matter of weeks after that and it was finished.

"Do I disagree with the book now? No, but remember in that book, I separate myself from middle-class women's organisations. Now they've been upset about that and they protested. They almost got me to the point where I was prepared to mitigate the severity of what I said about middle-class women in a new edition that was being prepared. But watching the way women screwed around over the Equal Rights Amendment here in America, I am convinced that middle-class white-collar women merely wish to be appointed to government committees and executive boards. I never wanted to talk about the ERA because I thought it was the most asinine idea from the beginning. How the fuck could they ever put that sort of thing in their Constitution? What kind of whitewashing is that? The only way a woman can live in America is by satisfying some man's concept of who he is. You've got to accompany a man everywhere. There is no separate life. You're not connected to other women. You don't live close to your mother-in-law, your mother, your sister, or any women. And academia is even worse than corporate life in that sense. Today, I am more interested in women in other countries who do have a female society, a society where they don't *have* to hang around with men all the time. And where they don't envy the lives men lead.

"I don't like living without a family for support. I hate giving everything to the IRS. Everyone I know is either married or dotty. I know a few bachelors but boy, they're a sorry lot. Bachelors of thirty-three and over are the most problematic section of the community. If you live my kind of life there are a lot of people around who are not committed to you. All kinds of relationship take precedence over your friendships. Marriage, you say, is a partnership. I have no principal objection to it as long as it doesn't masquerade as something else. As a consummation of the perfect love affair. It should be regarded as a businesslike arrangement, the basis of a household, a system for paying bills; it shouldn't be a romantic or sexual obsession.

"Australia? I had formed my plans to leave Australia when I was twelve. I think I decided that Australia and I were both deprived. It was boring. I used to walk down to Port Melbourne and watch the boats sail away, and I promised myself that I'd be on one just as soon as I could. It took me thirteen years to realise those plans. Once I'd gone, I knew I wasn't coming back. Now I don't go back because I couldn't earn a living in Oz. The Americans ask me to come and be a visiting professor all the time. Australia, never . . . forget it! I spoke four European languages before I was twelve. I used to pretend I was living in Europe. I thought that Europeans were much more beautiful than Australians. I don't think Australians are beautiful people. I do think the Italians are beautiful people. I would rather sit in a bar in Italy than swill champagne on the patio in Pymble surrounded by dentists and cosmetic surgeons telling me how long their boats are."

MAXWELL NEWTON

Amongst the great figures of Australian journalism stands Maxwell Newton. Apart from his editorships of the *Financial Review* and the *Australian*, he was a man who rolled dice with governments and affected the careers of prime ministers, Cabinet members and public servants. In one decade, he became a newspaper owner, a hopeless drunk, a bankrupt and, in final desperation, an operator of several sex-for-hire businesses in Melbourne's seedy massage-parlour industry.

He met his present wife, Olivia, who was also an alcoholic, when his fortunes were at their lowest ebb. Today, Newton, with the support of Olivia, is again plying his trade as a provocative financial columnist and author. Expatriation gave Newton an opportunity to wipe the slate clean and, at fifty-two, start again.

Max Newton was born in Perth in 1929, the son of English migrants. His father was a lead-burner in a sulphuric acid factory in Perth, and it was from him that young Max acquired the strong desire to be the top of the class — a desire which has dominated him throughout his career.

Newton attended Bayswater State School which provided public education up to the school-leaving age of twelve. The only way he could continue his education was by winning a scholarship to Perth Modern School, and from there hopefully move on to university. Obtaining a scholarship was tough. Most of the successful applicants, out of the many hundreds who sat for scholarship examinations, were prepared at two special cramming schools that catered mainly for the children of middle-class families. Mr Newton Sr managed to scrape up enough money to get his son tutored every Saturday morning for the scholarship examination. Newton just got in.

"My recollection of those years is one of fierce competition and tremendous striving for academic achievement. When you took your junior year, when you were fifteen, most people had their papers marked only up to the point where they passed. But at Perth Modern School, we used to pay extra and get our actual marks so we knew which kids in the class had actually done better. It wasn't a question of passing, it was a question of who won. The whole environment was one of ferocious competition. In my class, I was at the top, or near the top, a lot of the time."

The secretary of Newton's class was John Stone, at present the

---

Maxwell Newton, 1981 (ACP)

Secretary of a much bigger class, the Federal Treasury in Canberra. Another classmate was the former West Australian Labor senator and minister John Wheeldon, currently Foreign Editor of the *Australian*. Also in Newton's year was that "bumptious little bastard", Bob Hawke.

Newton did well at school. He finally left with exhibitions in English and history. He says the *crème de la crème* of the boys at Perth Modern were streamed into the science subjects, but Newton decided to study English, history, Latin, French and two units of maths, "with the girls". He also played hockey and was picked for the West Australian under-twenty-one team. Outside school, he studied typing, Esperanto, German and Russian, taking extra French at the Alliance Française. He won medals for French and Esperanto. He was an enthusiastic cadet-lieutenant in the school corps and in 1945, attended camp in Victoria at Puckapunyal, expecting to go into the army as an officer if the war continued. He was a prefect but "too unorthodox" to have been considered for school captain.

"I used to engage in tomfoolery with Jack Wheeldon ... like we used to get Hawke and put his legs underneath the iron legs of the desk and bend him back over and twist his arms round behind him and carry out a drum beat on his chest to get him into order. We used to put his books out the window and he'd have to get out on a two-storey window ledge to get them back. We tormented him.

"Another thing; all the kids were terrified about masturbating. Terrified. My father bought a book called *The Encyclopaedia of Sex Knowledge* and he hid it on the top of his wardrobe. My brother and I found it and I read every bloody comma about masturbation and I was the full bong on it and knew that it wasn't going to do anything to you. I used to conduct little seminars and tell these kids that there was nothing to worry about. I think I had a very material effect on the peace of mind of a whole generation of boys."

Newton's two exhibitions took him to St George's College at the University of Western Australia. In his first year at university he worked hard and got two A's and two B's. He got the B's in English and history: "Which is what I got the exhibitions in, so there obviously was something wrong." He took the line of least resistance and dumped English and history and concentrated on economics and French. Shortly after arriving at college, Newton showed the first indications of what was to be a lifelong problem for him: he started drinking heavily.

Newton struck up a friendship with an older student in the Economics Department, a man who was to have a considerable influence on him both intellectually and more seriously, he says, as a social role model. Austin Holmes had been a navigator in the RAAF and was studying under the Commonwealth Reconstruction and Training Scheme. Holmes later became a senior economist with the Reserve Bank, where he worked under "Nugget" Coombs, and was an important public official during the Whitlam years.

"In my first year, I was still acting like a schoolboy, underlining lots of stuff, reading lots of stuff, being terribly zealous and, in the end, no good. Aus told me that was ridiculous and suggested I go down to the pub and talk to him. He suggested I read a book called *The Art of Study* by a British psychologist named Mace. I did read it — it's only a thin book — and it was just like the whole world opened up, and I suddenly understood what it meant to be able to think. Aus taught me to think in terms of principles, to have a contempt for the examination system and to learn how to exploit it, which I did. I learnt to tip the exam questions and worked intensively three weeks a year just before them. It worked. I got A's all the way through."

However, Newton got a nasty shock when this system almost failed him in the final French examination. He took the exam, "... so drunk I could hardly write". He got a B. The result was a bitter disappointment, not only to Newton but to his teachers. His French record had been one of the best in Perth for years. Newton, not yet twenty-one, was becoming increasingly concerned about the demon which took him over when he drank and he was frightened where it might lead. One night, he took a girl to the riverfront and the next thing he recalls is walking through King's Park, five kilometres away, stark naked.

In his third year at the UWA, the contest for the Rhodes Scholarship was a two-horse race between Newton and his old school-chum John Stone. Both were considered, but Stone "walked away with it". Stone and Newton had lived together all through college but Newton, unlike Stone, was not considered "fit enough" to eat at the high table at St George's College. Although socially disabled by his drinking, Newton worked hard enough to win prizes in economics and French and got first-class honours. After a year's graduate work at the UWA, he was awarded a Hackett Studentship to attend an overseas university of his choice. He was accepted by Clare College, Cambridge, where his mentor Austin Holmes had preceded him the year before.

The scholarship arrived in the nick of time. Newton felt he had to get out of Perth. He felt very much the *"jeune homme des provinces"*. He stood on the platform of the Perth central railway station every night on his way home and watched the Westland express leave, wondering, "Will I ever get to the eastern States?"

The scholarship was worth £1000 for two years at the rate of £500 per annum. To conserve funds, it was important to get to England for as little as possible. His mother, who worked as a secretary for a legal firm in Perth, was finally able through her office to get Newton a job as a dishwasher on the SS *Otranto*.

"I worked that ship all the way to England and when I was paid off, I got £17 as wages. In between Fremantle and Tilbury, I washed something like 300,000 dishes. In the cabin on the *Otranto*, which I shared with seven other male members of the crew, I ended up acting as the mediator between my three other heterosexual cabinmates and 'Hilda', 'Delores', 'Jean' and 'Pam'."

Arriving in England months before the beginning of the university year, he got a job driving a tractor for a while, and then took off to the Sorbonne in Paris for a two-month course in French literature, grammar, and "purification of accent". Accent properly purified, Newton retired from Paris to a farm in Auvergne where he worked as a labourer, and then met up with an old friend in Marseilles who had also won a scholarship. The two Perth boys completed the final leg of their journey to Cambridge on a motorcycle.

The Max Newton who attended Clare College, Cambridge, was a very different man to the clever but contemptuous young soak who had bluffed his way to distinction in Perth:

"I never became involved in the life of the university, I did not drink, I did not smoke, I did not fool around. I did nothing but work or go to the pictures. My neighbour at Clare was Norman Podhoretz, and he and I in effect spent the whole year together sharing our coal and our food parcels. We never ate in hall, never really had anything to do with the young English at all — the young English gentlemen."

In England in the early 1950s, after almost a decade of the Welfare State, there was still egg, meat, and coal rationing. Newton's mother sent lots of tinned meat, especially tinned stew, which the Jewish-American Podhoretz had never tasted. Podhoretz's mother sent across whole tinned chicken and other exotic American tinned foods which Newton had never dreamed existed.

The relationship between Max Newton and Norman Podhoretz was more than a convenient pooling of resources. These two clever but slightly awkward colonials shared an aloofness — or sense of

As a student in Cambridge, early 1950s

insecurity perhaps — which prevented them joining the undernourished but gilded English youths at table or at play. Newton taught Podhoretz French, which was part of his course of study, and Podhoretz reciprocated by showing Newton: "... how it was possible to be honest in one's thinking. By the time I'd got to Cambridge, I'd developed some very nasty habits; contempt for any serious ideas, contempt for the educational system which I'd exploited for years, a gift for the slick answer."

Newton was supervised by a tutor called Brian Reddaway who specialised in applied economics. "I had to unlearn a lot of the old rubbish that I'd half-learned in Australia. I was able to con them in Western Australia. I couldn't con everybody at Cambridge. I got extra supervision from Joan Robinson. I was asked to be a member of a very elite group called the Political Economy Club, which Keynes had founded, and which was then run by a man called Dennis Robertson, who was Professor of Political Economy at Cambridge. I didn't work hard in the sense of working long hours, but what I did do I really tried to understand."

In 1952, at the end of his first year at Cambridge and aged twenty-three, Newton married Anne Kirby Robertson, a Perth girl he had met at the University of Western Australia and who had followed him to England, determined to marry him. The romance bloomed in England and Newton reciprocated Anne's desire for marriage.

To supplement Newton's scholarship, she took a job teaching at a school in Cambridge and they rented a large house just outside the town where they took in boarders. Newton obtained a summer job at Australia House working for Jim Nimmo, the Treasury representative, and commuted from Cambridge to London by train each day. He had received a bit of a jolt in the examination results at the end of the previous year. He narrowly missed a "first", and so his final year was really hard work.

"At the end of the year, I took the examinations and I nearly wrecked myself. I'd been nearly two years without a drink and the examinations were morning, afternoon, morning, afternoon, morning, afternoon, morning. Bang! That's it! Three and a half days and your life's finished. On the evening of the third day, there was a cocktail party given by the Master of my college and I had a few sherries and I got drunk and drank the whole bloody night. At four o'clock in the morning, I started vomiting and I was so ill I could hardly get up. Anne gave me a big packet of glucose and a big packet of Aspros and I told the invigilator on the final morning I was sick. Somehow I finished that examination. I got up every fifteen minutes, had a drink of water and some glucose and another Aspro. I was that crook. Skinned right down to the lean meat.

"A few weeks later, it was announced that I had got one of the two firsts that were given that year. I was given a thing called the Wrenbury Scholarship — it was for the outstanding economics graduate of the year — and was made an honorary scholar of Clare College. I was on top of the world. And once more top of the class."

Newton's college asked him to stay on and offered to find some money to provide him with a junior fellowship. By this time, however, "after seven years of exams", he was anxious to leave university life. He managed to get a job at Australia House in the Treasury section as a base-grade clerk. This was unheard of, an appointment to the Australian public service being made overseas. Additionally, it was rare in those days to appoint a graduate. He worked at Australia House for a year and saw all the cables coming in from Canberra.

After a year in London, the public service decided he should return to Canberra. By this time, Max and Anne had become the parents of a daughter — Sarah. The three Newtons embarked on the liner *Himalaya* at government expense and returned to Australia in comfort. The reception Newton received in Canberra was in some contrast to the ease of the leisurely trip home. The Treasury, concerned at the irregular manner in which Newton had been engaged and apprehensive of his superior qualifications, decided he must start at the very bottom of the totem pole. The work he was given to do was "meaningless".

As no housing was available, Newton and his family were first quartered in the Hotel Acton, a government hostel where the three of them lived in one room and ate in a cafeteria. Then the public service decided to move him to an even less comfortable hostel because Treasury officials decided that he was not "senior" enough for the Acton. They were allocated a room in an old fibro hostel:

"Our clothes were hung up on a bit of dowling with a curtain across. It was like living as a refugee and I dropped my bundle. I sat on the floor of our room each night with a flagon of sherry and just drank it. I had no prospects and it seemed to me that everything I'd done had been wasted. I was absolutely bewildered, confused and had completely lost my confidence."

Newton had met on the ship home a man called George Thompson who owned a company in Sydney called Marshall Batteries, which sold car batteries by mail-order. "I'd been getting £19 a week so I wrote to George. He wrote back and said I could have a job for £22 a week." Newton resigned from the Treasury and left for Sydney.

Although he did not stay long at the Treasury — a year in London and a year in Canberra — he did persuade an old classmate to join it: Rhodes Scholar John Stone. When Newton left London, Stone inherited his job at the Treasury section in London.

George Thompson lent the Newtons £3000 and they bought their first home in Harbord for £4500. "It was a terrible Sydney junk-built, mass-produced timber and fibro place, but to us it was like a dream come true." Newton, who by then was twenty-six years old and earning £22 a week, soon decided that he had to leave Marshall Batteries. He describes his sometime shipboard friend George Thompson as: "A terrible, tyrannical bloody bastard. Poor bugger, he died a few years later."

Newton wrote to the Bank of New South Wales. He was promptly interviewed and offered a job at £1200 a year and once again found himself with nothing to do, this time in the research department of Australia's oldest bank. "I wasn't allowed to do anything meaningful. I wasn't allowed to write anything. So I started my own battery business out in Harbord. I used to make batteries down in a shed at the back of the house with a blow-torch and acid and the rest of it, and sell them in the *Manly Daily*. I'd get up at about five o'clock and make the batteries and then come to work at the Bank of New South Wales and do nothing."

In 1956, Professor H. D. Arndt of the ANU had organised a group of economists to make a public statement calling on the government to take measures to fix the perennial balance of payments problems and get inflation under control. Having nothing else to do, Newton wrote a series of letters to the *Sydney Morning Herald* on this subject. All were published, bearing the signature Maxwell Newton, Harbord. Shortly after the fourth letter appeared, Newton received a telephone call from John Pringle, Editor of the *Herald*, asking him to come in to the office and see him. Pringle introduced him to Tom Fitzgerald, Financial Editor of the *Herald*, and they both arranged for him to meet Rupert Henderson, Managing Director of the Fairfax group.

Rupert Henderson told Newton: "I think you've got an outstanding future in journalism. What do they pay you at the Bank of New South Wales?" Max told him £30 a week. "Which was bullshit, I was getting £24. I was frightened that somehow they'd find out." Henderson offered him £40 a week. Newton somehow mustered the courage to reply, "Well, I've got very good prospects at the bank, Mr

Henderson. Can't you do any better than that?" Henderson replied that if Newton was any good, he would give him £50 a week in six months. "So off I went to the *Sydney Morning Herald*."

After a few months of kicking his heels in the corridors of the Fairfax building, he was sent to Canberra as the *Herald* political correspondent. The *Herald* had previously stationed in Canberra John Malone, who was the political correspondent for the newspaper, and a journalist called Roger Rae. Rae was the general reporter who did all the work; Malone was the great political writer who wrote "the piece" every week. Newton was meant to replace Malone, but nobody had indicated what Newton's standing or authority was.

For six months, Newton did virtually nothing. Finally, at Christmas, he went to Sydney and saw Fairfax's General Manager Angus MacLachlan and offered his resignation. But the canny MacLachlan refused to accept it and told Newton to take a month's holiday. When he returned, Pringle sent him back to Canberra promising that every Tuesday he would have an article in the *Herald*. From 1957 to 1960, Newton lived in Canberra with his family, writing for the *Herald* and doing the lead article for the *Financial Review* when it got going.

In 1958, Warwick Fairfax and Rupert Henderson decided to return to an old theme: the unhorsing of Robert Menzies, Australia's Liberal Prime Minister. The decision involved supporting the Opposition Leader, Dr H. V. Evatt, an erratically brilliant man whose mind was probably even then in the early stages of the debilitating disease that eventually ended his public life. Evatt (known as "The Doc") was given the full support of the Fairfax organisation in an attempt to bring down the Menzies government.

Max Newton's role in this was to act as speech-writer and *de facto* policy-maker for "The Doc". It must have been heady stuff for a young man who, a couple of years before, had been making batteries in his backyard and yawning through his days at the bank.

"During the 1958 election campaign, I was with 'The Doc' on the road. His mind had gone at that stage. It was so difficult to get any rational ideas across to him. I'd write articles for him about defence policy and economic policy, I'd write speeches for him about banking, and he'd go into Parliament and couldn't make a rational speech. Afterwards he'd say he was sorry. I would have to say to him: 'Look, Doc, if you don't bloody-well read what I give you, you're not going to get speeches, so you do what you're told.' It was quite obvious that Henderson saw me as someone who could be of great use to him in all sorts of ways, in writing speeches and creating policies."

In the 1961 election, Henderson instructed Newton to perform the same services for Arthur Calwell and Newton wrote almost all of the new Labor leader's important election speeches. Newton says Rupert Henderson said to him once: "If I told Arthur Calwell to stand on his head in the corner, he'd st-a-a-a-a-a-nd on his head in the corner."

"In Canberra, I was an innovator. I was one of the first journalists to penetrate the civil service. I ignored the politicians; they bored me. Alan Reid knew Roland Wilson and he knew Allen Brown and Jack Bunting [top echelon Departmental Secretaries] on a sort of Commonwealth Club level. But I knew the grubby little bastards down the line who were doing the dirty work and I got to know them very well and penetrated their whole setup. I knew from my experience in the Treasury that these officials were really the ones that ran the show and that they knew weeks and often months ahead of the ministers what was going on."

However, not all Newton's contacts were "grubby little bastards". He re-established old links at the Treasury, where he had started his career. "I was able to go back and interview people like Dick Randall [by then Deputy-Secretary of the Department]. I became friendly with Tom Strong, the head of the Bureau of Agricultural Economics. He was really the one who opened my eyes to Alan Westerman and the whole of his Department of Trade apparatus. Alf Rattigan, when he was Chairman of the Tariff Board, was tremendously helpful to me.

"One official I got very involved with was Don Anderson, the Director of Civil Aviation. The two-airline policy was evolving at that time. I became almost a member of the civil aviation apparatus. They used to show me draft bills before they went to the minister, they'd show me their internal documents, and I reported their side of the story and was materially a part of the whole campaign. These issues included stopping TAA getting the Caravelle; trying to stop Ansett from getting the Electra; trying to force them both to take the Viscount 800; stopping Vicker's from selling one of their big terrible models to Qantas."

In 1960, Newton was asked to come back to Sydney and take over direction of the *Financial Review*, as Managing Editor. In typical Fairfax fashion, Harry Williams, the Editor, remained. Newton finally worked out a *modus vivendi* with Williams which gave him control of the staff and the stories, while Williams processed the copy. The

Newspaper editor, 1969 (News Ltd)

Financial Review was still a weekly with a circulation of 9000. Within two years of Newton's arrival, the circulation had more than doubled to about 20,000, and Newton was pushing management to make it a bi-weekly with publication on Tuesdays and Thursdays.

He became quite theatrical in some of his confrontations with the Fairfax management. There were "... huge rows, sulking, carryings-on and my usual appalling bloody behaviour". However, one thing Newton was not doing during that period was drinking. He had had a nasty shock when he came back from Canberra in 1960. His wife Anne wanted to leave him and go back to Canberra to live with a diplomat from what was then appropriately called the Department of External Affairs. "I pleaded with her, I got down on my knees and I said that if you don't go I will not drink again. And I did not drink again for the whole time that I was with her, during the whole of our subsequent ten years together."

Newton recalls of that period: "OK, so here I am, I'm not drinking, I'm really charging. The *Financial Review* is going like a rocket. My prestige in the building is high. But I've still got problems. Angus Edward Upjohn Maude [an Englishman imported by Fairfax] is now Editor of the *Sydney Morning Herald* and has got the right of veto over my leaders in the *Financial Review*, which I detest! This was the Fairfax 'thing' — the Editor of the *Sydney Morning Herald* controlled all thinking in the entire organisation. Everything — the *Sun-Herald*, the *Sun, Pix-People, Radio, Television and Hobbies*, the *Financial Review* — all came under the Editor of the *Sydney Morning Herald* who was the fountain of all policy thinking, because he was Warwick's chosen instrument. I had a fearsome guerrilla war with Maude. He used to like to go out and have a long dinner, come back three-parts shickered and I was supposed to have a galley [proof] of the *Financial Review* leader ready for him to see."

Newton would not cooperate. He would put the galley-proofs of the editorials under the wrong door, or wait until one in the morning to send them up to Maude, hoping he had gone home. "At one stage, I got so enraged with Maude having anything to do with anything that I did that I said to Jules Zanetti, the chief subeditor at the *Financial Review*, 'Get last week's leader and put another head on it and see if they notice the difference'. Well, they didn't. It was pathetic."

What he did do was tighten up the deadlines and get the paper out on time. "When I came there they couldn't get the bloody thing out until two o'clock in the morning; a twenty-eight-page paper! I got it back to quarter past twelve and that allowed us to catch planes to

Melbourne and Brisbane. I got really involved in the close management of the paper. It was exciting." The *Financial Review* went bi-weekly, sales rose to 28,000 and it started to attract a lot more advertising.

In 1962 and 1963, Newton had problems with Warwick Fairfax and Rupert Henderson over editorial policy. Fairfax believed Britain should join the Common Market and that his papers should support Britain's entry: "At that stage, I was close to Jack McEwen and against both Menzies and Warwick on that issue. I believed that it would be very bad for Australia if Britain went into the Common Market."

He also believed strongly that Australia needed some sort of restrictive trade practices legislation and Fairfax hated the thought of it. Newton frequently published articles in the *Financial Review* advocating viewpoints opposed to Warwick Fairfax's policies.

However, he was sent to London, in 1962, for the meeting of the Commonwealth Prime Ministers on Britain's proposed entry into the Common Market. Jack McEwen briefed him each day in his room at the Savoy Hotel. Newton and McEwen were working together, trying to ensure that Menzies did not support Britain's application to the Common Market. On this issue, Newton, as a Fairfax editor, was opposing his proprietor's policy and McEwen, as a senior minister in the Menzies Cabinet, was opposing his Prime Minister. Co-conspirators indeed!

In the end, they won that battle. Menzies, the last great Australian imperialist, told the conference, chaired by Harold MacMillan, that the British should not ally themselves in the Common Market with the Europeans whose ideas of democracy were both recent and sketchy. These remarks were made in closed conference, but Menzies later released the text of his speech to the press.

Once more, this was heady stuff for Newton: "Menzies went over to Jack's [McEwen] side and dumped MacMillan which was a bloody sensation ... and, of course, in the background, Jack's main ally was Beaverbrook who had the imperial lady in chains on the masthead of the *Daily Express*."

However, his role in persuading Australia to oppose Britain's entry into the Common Market was another case of winning the battle and losing the war. Britain did, of course, enter the Common Market and for Max Newton his London trip represented the high-water of his relationship with Jack McEwen. Like so many of Newton's former associates, he was destined to become a bitter and implacable enemy.

Newton found himself arguing with management, not only on

matters of editorial policy, but also on the future of the *Financial Review*. He spent most of 1963 persuading Henderson and MacLachlan that the paper was ready to be turned into a daily like the *Wall Street Journal* (which appears every day the Stock Exchange is open). After a false start in August which was aborted when news of the change was leaked without Henderson's approval, the *Financial Review* finally became a daily in October 1963. The price was held at one shilling and sales settled at 19,000. The Fairfax management refused to drop the cover price to sixpence. Newton disagreed at the time, but when he published his own papers he became just as fond of high cover prices.

In 1963, the old Liberal warhorse Robert Menzies took to the campaign trail for his last election. At Fairfax headquarters, there was a rare division of opinion between the laird, Warwick Fairfax, and his steward, Rupert Henderson. Warwick Fairfax had married his third wife, Mary Symonds, a socially ambitious woman, in 1959. Mary was to have a great influence on Warwick. By 1963, she was almost certainly waiting for the happy day when the gates of Buckingham Palace would open to them both and her aging husband would bend his knee to the Queen and rise, making her a Lady. Apart from this, that great national barometer of prosperity, the classified columns of the *Sydney Morning Herald*, was bulking up after some lean times in 1961 and 1962. The Fairfax patrimony was safe again. The upshot of all this was that Warwick wanted the Menzies government returned. Henderson, on the other hand, probably felt that by this time he had a considerable investment in Arthur Calwell, and no doubt hoped that a Labor government would rearrange the television licensing system in a manner more suited to the Fairfax interests. Had Arthur Calwell won the 1963 elections, Rupert Henderson would have been the *eminence grise* of the new government.

Max Newton was instructed by Henderson to continue supporting Calwell, both editorially in the *Financial Review* and by assisting with the planning of policies and the writing of election addresses. He worked closely with the ALP's advertising agency, McCann-Erickson, and with Arthur Calwell himself. However, seven days before the election, Warwick Fairfax intervened and caused an editorial to be published in the *Sydney Morning Herald* headed "Why the Government Should Be Returned". This was repeated in the *Sun-Herald* the next day as an editorial, despite the not inconsiderable

Commonwealth police search Maxwell Newton's files, Canberra, 1969 (ACP)

news of the assassination of President Kennedy in Dallas, Texas, the day before.

That Monday, before the election, a gloomy quartet of Fairfax executives, including Newton, met in Henderson's office to assess the damage. Newton remembers Henderson asking him: "Well, what do you think about it all now, Mr Newton?" Newton said: "I feel sick ... What's going to happen when Mr Fairfax gets his knighthood?" Henderson replied: "Then my humiliation will be complete." But Henderson's humiliation had to wait another four years. Menzies won the '63 election handily and retired without knighting Warwick Fairfax. That distinction fell to Sir Robert Askin, a man who was later to be accused on his deathbed of personal corruption by a Fairfax publication.

The split in the office affected Newton's enthusiasm for his job. Early in 1964, he sought out Rupert Murdoch who told him that he was looking for an editor for a daily paper he intended to start up in competition to the *Canberra Times*, to be called the *Australian*. Newton resigned, taking with him a number of journalists for the new paper from the *Sydney Morning Herald* and its associated publications. However, Henderson was far from idle. He activated a secret agreement with Arthur Shakespeare to purchase the *Canberra Times* and quickly changed it from a sleepy provincial paper into a more ambitious broadsheet, thus undermining Murdoch's market in Canberra.

Thus checked by Henderson, Newton and Murdoch were forced to make the *Australian* a national paper produced from Canberra. This caused Murdoch tremendous problems, and put his group into a trading loss, something he had told the Commonwealth Bank (which was supporting him) would not happen. The pressure had its effect on the relationship between Newton and Rupert Murdoch. Newton would last as a Murdoch editor for just under a year.

"Rupert and I drifted apart. Rupert became more worried about his business. He became suspicious of me, I think, because of my connections with the Treasury. He was very deeply involved with Jack McEwen then. He supported protectionism, he supported many Left-Liberal causes. He was violently opposed to the war in Vietnam which I thought was a very important thing for Australia. I remember recommending that we support the bombing of Haiphong Harbour. Rupert was appalled ... I don't blame him for being frightened; he had bloody good reason to be frightened. About the middle of 1965, an agreement was reached that I quit."

For the first time in his life, Newton, aged thirty-six, was unemployed. He owned a 1958 Holden, had £3000 in the bank and was living in a house in Canberra owned by Murdoch which he would soon have to vacate. He had a wife and three children to support. He persuaded Staniforth Ricketson of the Melbourne brokerage firm of J. B. Were to pay him £2000 a year to produce a weekly Canberra letter for the firm and its clients. He became a stringer, paid only when his work appeared, for the London *Economist*, the *Financial Times* and *Time* magazine. He found it impossible to make any real money.

In some desperation, he started a newsletter, *Incentive*, dealing with economic policy and politics and charged $30 for an annual subscription. At its peak, the letter had 800 subscribers and became extremely profitable. Newton bought a house in the Canberra suburb of Deakin and later put a deposit on the house next door which he turned into an office.

He then bought the *Management Newsletter* from the firm of W. D. Scott and Co. and also contracted to write Scott's economic advisory letter to their clients. Within two years of leaving the *Australian* in May 1965, Newton was grossing in excess of $100,000 a year and his only significant expense was postage. At about this time, Massey Stanley, a former journalist doing public relations work for Japanese interests in Australia, asked Newton to write a newsletter about tariff developments for the Japanese External Trade Organisation known as JETRO.

Another important contact was made early in 1967, when Newton's old chum Sim Rubensohn, boss of McCann-Erickson (the agency which produced Labor's advertising in the '59, '61 and '63 elections), introduced him to one of the agency's clients, Dick Crebbin, the Chairman of Marrickville Holdings Ltd, who was trying to get restrictions on margarine production in Australia abolished. Newton says of this relationship: "I gradually came to have a very important role in that company. I wrote their annual reports, but more importantly, I became very much involved in the campaign to have margarine quotas abolished."

Newton worked closely with the advertising agency in developing the famous "Mrs Jones campaign" which he describes as being about freedom of choice. He also wrote a pamphlet entitled *The Great Dairy Hoax* which was distributed in every dairy-producing electorate in Australia. This booklet claimed that the poorer dairy farmers in Queensland and New South Wales were not getting a fair share of the dairy subsidy, the bulk of which went to the richer Victorian dairy farmers who didn't need it anyway.

Newton was obviously on a collision course with Jack McEwen, the Deputy Prime Minister and head of the Country Party. Newton supported lower tariffs in general in his various newsletters and articles. Traditionally, one would have expected the Country Party to support free trade but McEwen's contribution to his party was to haul aboard its creaking hull Australia's high tariff manufacturers.

The last straw for McEwen was the active role Newton played in the denigration of the Vernon Report, which was largely inspired by Sir John Crawford, the permanent head of McEwen's department. The report proposed the shift of economic policy-making from the Treasury to a new economic policy secretariat which would have inevitably been dominated by McEwen and Crawford.

The Treasury gave John Stone the task of conducting the campaign against the Vernon Report. Newton at that time was writing a fortnightly column for a small but influential magazine called *Nation*. He used this column and his newsletters to attack the Vernon Report and the people behind it. The campaign was successful. The Vernon Report was consigned to a Canberra pigeonhole. The Treasury had survived and McEwen had yet another reason to hate Max Newton's guts.

In 1966, William McMahon, known to all and sundry as "Billy", became Federal Treasurer. His years as Treasurer probably represent the best of McMahon as an effective politician. He was temperamentally and ideologically in agreement with his Treasury officials — for McMahon a rare state of affairs. He recognised in McEwen not only a philosophical opponent but also an eventual rival for the Prime Ministry.

He also got on well with Max Newton. Newton's convictions were well known and they had attracted clients who felt they could profit by them. McMahon regularly attacked McEwen's proposals in Cabinet. The Treasury Department itself, allegedly above politics but still smarting from the McEwen-Crawford take-over bid, did what it could to denigrate suggestions originating from McEwen's Trade Department or any other Country Party department. Newton became the house publicist for these points of view.

McMahon started toting Newton around with him wherever he went. On one occasion, Newton was arrested in Trinidad at a Commonwealth Finance Ministers' conference for swiping a British working paper and was going to be thrown off the island. McMahon interceded and had him released. On another occasion, McMahon took Newton along to a private dinner of Commonwealth Finance

Ministers held in Montreal, an action Newton describes as slightly "scandalous".

This was the state of affairs when Harold Holt went for a pre-Christmas swim in 1967 and failed to come back. As his deputy in the Liberal Party, Billy McMahon was expected to succeed him. McEwen crushed this hope by announcing that if McMahon was chosen Leader of the Liberal Party, the Country Party would not serve under him in a coalition government, one reason being that McMahon was under the influence of the evil Maxwell Newton.

Rupert Murdoch's *Australian* picked this story up and Newton became a notorious public figure. John Gorton became Prime Minister (after Jack McEwen's caretaker month in office following Holt's disappearance) instead of McMahon, and relationships between Newton and Billy cooled suddenly as Billy distanced himself from the man who seemed to have cost him his shot at the top job.

Then followed a period of official harassment for Newton. "During this time I had various officials in the government working for me. They used to give me copies of documents and I paid them. I had a sort of a milkrun. I'd go round on Saturday morning and poke cheques underneath their doormats and pick up envelopes."

One of Newton's paid informants was an employee in the Department of Trade who copied cables and gave them to Newton, who published them. "Not that they were important, but it gave me more notoriety." One cable, which Newton published in full, was a report of a conversation between the then Australian Ambassador to France and General De Gaulle.

Publication of this cable gave McEwen an excuse to ask Gorton for a Commonwealth police raid on Newton's office and home. Fourteen Commonwealth policemen in plain clothes duly raided both of Newton's houses in Deakin, examining every scrap of paper on the premises. "It took them about twelve hours to go through the two places and they eventually found a hand-written note from this guy in the Department of Trade. They were able to trace him and he was tipped out of the public service." Newton's lawyers took immediate action against the Commonwealth government for illegal search and seizure on the basis that the search-warrant was invalid. To the intense annoyance of the government, Mr Justice Fox in the ACT Supreme Court upheld Newton's claim, ending any prospect of a Commonwealth prosecution.

Frustrated in his attempt to have Newton charged with a criminal offence, McEwen then attempted to have him evicted from the parliamentary press gallery on the grounds that he was engaged in non-journalistic political and propaganda activities in Parliament House. This failed when journalists who had worked with Newton in the past revealed to the other members of the gallery that McEwen had promised them preferential information if they voted to kick Newton out.

About this time, Newton bought a couple of country newspapers in New South Wales which he was printing from a factory in Fyshwick, Canberra. He started a weekly mining newspaper, called the *Australian Miner*, and he bought *Jobson's Investment Digest*. Marrickville Holdings financed most of this expansion. It also financed the acquisition of the *Daily Commercial News*, a faltering shipping newspaper published in all mainland capital cities. Newton turned this into a profitable operation by printing it in one location and using a computer to collate shipping movements and traffic. It was the first shipping paper in the world to do so.

However, Newton's problems with the Federal government had not ended. There were still visits from police, knocks on the door at night and constant attempts to close him down. "I used to print the ANU student newspaper. In one of their issues they had silhouettes showing the forty-eight positions of coitus. When I printed this, my opponents tried to have me closed up under the ACT Printing Ordinance. They abandoned that idea as well. Gradually the pressure dropped off."

Newton says that he is convinced that the reason for the abatement of the harassment was his public announcement that he had a statutory declaration from Geraldine Willesee locked in a safe deposit box. In this document, Willesee was supposed to have sworn to what had actually happened during an incident between Prime Minister Gorton and herself which had become the subject of considerable public and private speculation. "Gorton, I think, felt the need to steer a bit clear of me. Subsequently, in about 1979, he even publicly stated that I was the cause of his downfall."

McEwen went so far as to accuse Newton of spying. "He said in Parliament that I was a Japanese spy." He claimed that Newton had signed a contract with the Japanese to engage in commercial espionage. "I was able to counter that by producing the actual contract that I had with JETRO."

Another attempt by McEwen to discredit Newton involved his campaigning against margarine quotas. Newton had contracted some printing for Marrickville Margarine to another printer in Canberra. When Newton took this business away, the other printer objected and took an old cheque from Marrickville Holdings to McEwen. "Jack waved this cheque around Parliament House, saying it was a cheque for $30,000 to pay for the printing of *The Great Dairy Hoax*." Fortunately for Newton, McEwen had been given the wrong cheque. It was to pay for advertising pamphlets for a completely unrelated new product that Marrickville Holdings was launching. "It wasn't that they weren't on the right track, it was just that they were incompetent. And it was the same with the coppers; they were incompetent. And so I was saved . . ."

Newton described how his encounters with the police typically proceeded: "The coppers would open up a conversation and say, 'Is your name Maxwell Newton?' I'd say: 'Acting on legal advice, I decline to answer that question.' At one stage, I was in my lawyer's office with a policeman for three and a half hours and I answered every question along those lines. I found that once I did that, they didn't know what to do. Their main method of attack was (and is) to get the accused person to confess or make a mistake."

Newton had given up alcohol in 1960 and did not drink again until the early 1970s. He finally became very unsettled by the strain of the constant police harassment and his doctor prescribed Valium and Mandrax. He soon became addicted to both. He describes Mandrax as "more lethally addictive than heroin". For a period of several years, Newton was unable to walk around without a plentiful supply of both drugs. He became a frightened person and couldn't sleep. "A lot of my emotional immaturity and my neurotic behaviour became more pronounced."

In 1970, Newton found out that Gordon Barton was going to close his *Sunday Observer*, leaving Melbourne without a Sunday paper. To produce a Sunday paper in Melbourne, Newton needed independent distribution into the sub-agents which stayed open on Sundays to sell the Sydney Sunday papers. This he got from Consolidated Press, which at that stage was distributing the *Sunday Telegraph* in Melbourne. Armed with his distribution agreement, he arranged financing from his old chum Dick Crebbin at Marrickville Holdings. One week after the Barton-owned *Sunday Observer* closed, Newton was ready to start up with a paper called the *Melbourne Observer*. Barton attempted to protect the title but failed in court, and finally Newton even changed the name of his paper to the *Sunday Observer*.

During the balance of 1970 and 1971, the *Sunday Observer* staggered along. Newton and his wife Anne were starting to feel the strain of the past ten years. He had a new wing built on his house in

Canberra with a bedroom and a bathroom and a connecting door to the rest of the house. Newton would lock himself in for days at a time, alone with his bottles of Mandrax. When not freaked out on drugs, he was endlessly commuting between Canberra, Brisbane, Sydney and Melbourne.

While in Melbourne, he started seeing Diane Austin whom he had met in 1970. In 1972, he asked her to accompany him on a trip to Japan. In Hong Kong, Newton was so consumed with guilt about deceiving Anne, he took an "enormous" dose of Mandrax and was unconscious for two days in the Mandarin Hotel. When he and Diane finally got to Japan, he started drinking, something he had not done since 1960.

Later in 1972, he left Anne and the children in Canberra and moved in with Diane in Melbourne. The *Sunday Observer* increasingly became his preoccupation to the exclusion of all else. There was a Federal election at the end of 1972. The big news for most people was that after almost twenty-five years out of office, Labor had won. The outgoing Prime Minister was Newton's old buddy Billy McMahon. But what Newton remembers about the election is that for the first time his paper sold more than 100,000 copies.

The relationship between Max Newton and Dick Crebbin, of Marrickville Holdings, was a close one. Newton attended board meetings, where he discussed the *Sunday Observer* and the *Daily Commercial News* as if they were divisions or subsidiaries. Marrickville financed Newton's various acquisitions in the newspaper field. Newton says he felt they wanted investments outside the food business. However, Newton's unpredictable and erratic behaviour during 1972 and 1973 finally soured this relationship too. In 1974, there was a parting of interests. Marrickville took over sole control of the *Daily Commercial News*, leaving Newton alone with his beloved *Sunday Observer*.

These were bad years for Newton. He was back on the booze and still taking large quantities of Mandrax. He would sometimes stop at a pub on his way to work and fortify himself with half a dozen brandies laced with lime and soda. At the end of the day, he would often drink a dozen beers and then might or might not go home. Living in a largish house in Baxter Street, Toorak, and driving a Rolls Royce, Newton was putting on a brave front to the world, but his relationship with Diane was seriously affected by his drinking and he

With Olivia on their wedding day, 1981

was constantly attacked by acute bouts of depression and fear. He remained extremely remorseful about ending his marriage to Anne who was a good friend to him and "never did me any wrong at all".

In July 1973, Newton checked into the Town House Motel with five dozen cans of beer, six bottles of Scotch and 100 Mandrax. He consumed the lot and lay unconscious for two days. When he awoke, he was very weak but managed to ring Diane. She came with a friend and took him to a private hospital which specialised in the treatment of alcoholism.

After a few days, he recovered and slipped out of the hospital. "I used to walk around the place with my dressing-gown on. So I got fully dressed underneath my dressing-gown, jumped over the back fence, chucked my dressing-gown back and was off. I went to the Southern Cross in Melbourne, checked in (I was well known there) ordered a bottle of Scotch and was lying on the bed when they caught up with me again. This time they brought a guy called Teddy with them, who was in Alcoholics Anonymous, and Ted became my sponsor."

This time Newton stayed in hospital. When he was released, he joined Alcoholics Anonymous and spent a lot of time at their meetings. Soon after, in July 1973, he threw away his drugs and has not used them since. "I also chucked out all the fear; it went out of my life. It was a fantastic relief."

Newton was printing 120,000 papers each Saturday night on a variety of baby presses scattered through the suburbs. The Melbourne *Herald* and the *Age*, acting in unholy alliance, had decided to produce a joint Sunday paper in opposition to Newton's. He was concerned that the Melbourne *Herald* would put pressure on these small suburban companies not to print his paper. To protect himself he needed a press. So in late 1973, Newton took over Regal Press, which gave him the printing capacity he needed to print the *Observer* on his own. He added extra equipment and improved the paper considerably. By Grand Final weekend in 1974, it was selling 200,000 copies a week at a cover price of forty cents.

However, like most publishers who buy a press to print a weekly newspaper, Newton faced the problem of keeping it busy on the six days of the week when the *Observer* wasn't published. He acquired the rights to a line of American comics and arranged distribution through a company jointly owned by Fairfax interests and the English IPC group. Unfortunately, it was decided to dissolve the company and the distribution organisation was wound up. This left Newton with thousands of comics out in the market-place and no way of collecting what was owing to him.

Short of money, he borrowed a million dollars from the Farmers' and Graziers' Cooperative through its Chairman, Les Smart. (As a result of making this loan, Les Smart was convicted of illegal disbursement of funds. He spent about six months in gaol before being awarded a new trial. He was acquitted late in 1982. Max Newton gave evidence for Smart in his second trial in New York to Barrister Kerry Milte QC, who came from Melbourne to take it.)

The loan did not staunch the flow. The overheads were large and, apart from the *Sunday Observer*, profitable jobbing work was impossible to get. Finally, in 1975, Newton appointed a receiver to try to get the place reorganised on a profitable basis. He was still employed by the receiver to run the business and actively sought additional capital to keep the *Sunday Observer* alive, and claims to have paid in to the receiver $500,000, mainly in cash raised from Melbourne doctors.

In April 1976, the receiver sent Newton a notice of dismissal from his job as manager of the *Sunday Observer* by telegram. The party was over. He had been thrown out of his own company.

Newton was now unemployed and broke, living in a Toorak house he could not afford to pay off. His Rolls Royce had been repossessed. However, the building society "couldn't evict me from this house for some reason, or else they were too embarrassed. They had given me a loan to buy it for about a quarter of a million dollars. It was like a contra-loan. The interest was 'contraed' off in ads in the *Sunday Observer*. This house was known as 'Contra Castle' because it was largely furnished and rebuilt on the contra."

Finally, in 1977, Newton "decamped" from the house. He and Diane took a rented house in Kooyong. They had by now two girls: Natasha and Sally. They had married in April 1975 and the Melbourne *Truth* ran a photograph showing Newton getting into the wedding car formally attired in evening clothes with Diane in her bridal dress, and told its readers: "We hope the bride has got some money because the bridegroom hasn't got enough to pay the wedding bill."

At this stage of his career, Newton became the publisher of a number of pornographic newspapers, having already provided printing facilities for a number of pornographic publications on his press at the *Sunday Observer*. He published these papers in Melbourne and distributed them in both Sydney and Melbourne.

"All this time, from 1974 to 1977, I'd been consistently unfaithful to Diane. I was in AA, I didn't take any drugs, but it was as if indiscriminate sex was like a relief somehow. I could lose myself in wild sex. Diane became very preoccupied about that, understandably. One of the women I became involved with was Olivia. I met her through an ad she placed in one of the sex papers I owned."

Newton's new business prospered. Soon he was wholesaling as well as retailing. He opened a mail-order business which received a set-back when Rupert Murdoch found out that Newton was placing ads in his Sydney papers and squashed them, costing Newton something like $5000 a week in lost sales. By the end of 1978, he was back in Toorak. "I had a pornographic shop in Melbourne, I had a mail-order business in Melbourne selling pornographic books and sex aids, and I was making a living. I could have survived."

In October 1977, Newton, on the advice of an accountant, had voluntarily filed for personal bankruptcy. This attracted the attention of the Income Tax Commissioner. "They had two men investigating me for two years trying to find out where I'd hidden 'the money'. They came to me in 1976 and said: 'You've understated your income by six hundred and something thousand dollars and we want $380,000. If you give us a cheque now that'll be OK.'

"I said: 'You can go to the shithouse, you will get nothing from me. I will give you nothing.' And they've never got anything. They were very angry about that. They briefed a QC to represent them at my bankruptcy hearing. The tax people kept saying: 'This man must pay, he's got it somewhere.' They never found it. Needless to say, it wasn't there to be found."

In 1978, Newton sent Diane and Natasha on a three-week trip to America. Sally stayed with friends. Newton spent each evening with Olivia, returning home each night in time for Diane's regular call. She was checking up on his whereabouts. This was virtually the end of Max's relationship with Diane. Within two weeks of her return to Melbourne, she caught Newton and Olivia *in flagrante delicto* and told Newton to get out.

Stunned, Newton moved in with Olivia "for a few days". He asked for and received a lot of help in the early days of his separation from Diane. He haunted AA meetings whenever he could. He was desperate about not seeing his daughters Sally and Natasha every day. Olivia, also an AA member, helped him a great deal.

About a year or so later, Newton had a breakthrough in the development of his recovery through AA. One of the steps towards recovery in that organisation's programme involves both "surrender of self" and acceptance of a "greater power or being". Newton says he accepted (if that is the right word) the "higher power" requirement in 1979. Interestingly, it was that year that his career as a financial journalist started to pick up again.

In the meantime, there were bills to be paid and money to be earned. When Newton left Diane, he abandoned the businesses he was then operating as they were in Diane's name. Using Olivia's name, Newton and Olivia opened three new sex businesses in Melbourne. These were more hard core and included massage parlours and pornography shops. They were highly lucrative. The weekly takings eventually grew to about $12,000. They were able to move to more comfortable quarters in Toorak. Olivia's sister Jo moved in with them and he bought a new car. Newton was able to see Natasha and Sally occasionally.

In 1979, Mark Day, the Editor of the new Australian *Penthouse*, asked Newton to write a political article on the Whitlam years for the first issue. For the first time in ten years, Newton had to sit down and write properly again. He went to the Melbourne Public Library and caught up with all the economic statistics he had ignored for the past decade. He enjoyed it, and Day asked him to write more articles.

John Singleton, who was running a sort of interview programme on Sydney's Channel Ten at that time, asked Newton to become a permanent guest. Newton and Olivia commuted to Sydney each week for Newton's TV appearances.

Then, surprisingly, his path crossed Rupert Murdoch's again. Murdoch attempted to take over the Herald and Weekly Times group, parent company of the Melbourne *Herald*, and the ABC asked Newton to comment on this in a public affairs programme, no doubt assuming that Newton, as a sacked Murdoch editor, would attack the proposal. To their surprise, Newton supported Murdoch's bid, saying it could only invigorate the newspapers concerned. Murdoch wrote thanking Newton and suggested dinner. A series of dinners followed at the Melbourne Hilton, in which Newton unburdened himself to Murdoch, telling him all that had happened to him in the last ten years. Murdoch confided in Newton in return, and he discovered that Murdoch had become a good deal more conservative than he was in the days when Newton was editing the *Australian*.

Murdoch asked Newton to write regularly for the *Australian* and Newton enthusiastically agreed. Shortly afterwards, Murdoch asked Newton to send him fortnightly reports advising him on the policies his Australian papers should follow. Newton sent these reports off for a while and then suggested that Murdoch should write a series of signed articles stating his views about Australia. Newton would work on the articles with him and research the information needed.

Murdoch agreed and asked Newton, accompanied by Olivia, to fly to New York to prepare the series. They left Australia in mid-1980.

When they arrived in New York, Murdoch decided not to proceed with the articles but asked Newton to stay on there as a financial columnist for his *New York Post*. Newton now contributes regularly as well to the *Times* of London, the *Australian* and Murdoch's other Australian papers. In January 1983, New York Times Books published his first book, *The Fed*, a trenchant attack on the American central bank. As a result of *The Fed* Max has become a popular public speaker at hard money gatherings.

Newton and Olivia were married in November 1981. They live fifty kilometres from New York in a charming Connecticut village and count their blessings:

"I thought that by having my own publications, I'd have more power. I had none. No influence. Back in the '60s, I thought, 'Well, I've got newsletters, but I'll get much better when I've got newspapers'. I had much more influence when I had newsletters. The power of ideas is much greater than the power of circulation in many ways. Since I came here, I've had the most exciting, happiest and productive time of my life.

"I don't want to have anything to do with Australia in the way of going back there. There are so many nasty things there relating to me. I went through a period from 1968 to 1978 of virtually permanent disaster, fear, personal catastrophe, bankruptcy, the police, the bloody tax people, public humiliation; a ten-year mid-life crisis.

"Since I've come to America, I've been able to work with people who take me at my face value. If I do good work, people are happy about it. Most people want to help me. In Australia, what I found is that if I did good work, people would be angry about it.

"When Milton Friedman wrote me last year praising my book [*The Fed*], I said to Olivia: 'That is the ultimate praise I can get. If I died now, nobody could have said anything better about my work.' I thought: 'I've been given this fantastic prize — Milton Friedman says my work is outstanding. Now where do we go?'

"In the old days, I would have thought: 'There's only one thing to do and that's die.' I used to go and get drunk. It was as if I could smash myself down so that I could start again and hit another pinnacle. Throughout a lot of my life, I've destroyed things, more or less smashed them, so I could start again somehow."

Financial columnist, *New York Post*, 1981 (ACP)

ZOE CALDWELL

I caught up with Zoe Caldwell and her husband Robert Whitehead when they were visiting Santa Barbara to see Dame Judith Anderson. They were staying in the guesthouse of a large but gloomy Montecito estate of Italian pretensions. We lunched together under the watchful eyes of Dame Judith, and then Caldwell and I talked.

Caldwell's domestic and maternal instincts have always dominated her love for the theatre. Had she not sometimes allowed her thespian skills to lie dormant, she might have become a fabulously rich actress and totally neurotic woman. Her strong commitment to family is a quality she inherited from her own mother, and which she hopes to pass onto her own children.

Caldwell was born in Melbourne in 1933 at the height of the Depression. Her father, Edgar Caldwell, a semi-invalid from the First World War, had lost his plumbing business and his house in Elsternwick and been forced to move his family to Moir Street, Glenferrie. Zoe Caldwell's mother, born Zoe Weil Hivon, had tripped the boards in her youth, touring the Far East in an Australian Gilbert and Sullivan company. History does not record whether this company had the audacity to perform *The Mikado* in Japan.

The elder Zoe had retired from the theatre shortly after reaching puberty, shocked at the general state of immorality existing within it. Now, during the Depression, she was forced to return to public entertainment to support the family. She was employed as a hostess at the Hawthorn dance studio of Percy Silk. Shortly after she started work here, her husband was also employed by the ballroom as a dinner-jacketed ticket-taker.

The kindly Percy Silk obviously liked the Caldwells and lent them his beach cottage for a brief holiday. It was there, claims Caldwell, that she was conceived. She was twelve years younger than her brother. Before she was three, Caldwell was mimicing Mae West's "Come up and see me sometime" and singing "A Tisket A Tasket".

Caldwell learned tap and ballet from Doris Gee and went to Vera Hopton to do eurhythmics and dance, and to learn to sing. There were lots of dancing and tap contests, lots of medals won. After a while, Caldwell's mother began to get apprehensive about the wicked theatre again, and the prospect of her daughter growing up to

---

Zoe Caldwell, Melbourne Theatre Company, 1983 (News Ltd)

become part of that world, but it was then discovered that Caldwell suffered from what is now called small motor skills learning disability. In plain English, it meant she lacked manual dexterity. What she was gifted in was the "large motor skill" stuff involving full, free body movement. It was decided it would be unwise to interfere with her course of studies as she was progressing so well.

When Caldwell was seven, a relative died in Lancashire and left a legacy. The family were able to leave Glenferrie for the more salubrious surroundings of Balwyn.

"Suddenly we were in a house. We had a vacuum cleaner and I had my own bedroom. My dad got a job with the Box Hill Gas Company as a gas-fitter and plumber, so he was able to leave Percy Silk's ballroom and become a feller in his own right."

Caldwell transferred to Balwyn State School but felt she did not belong there. She did not get on with fellow students or staff. Finally, at age twelve, she went to the Methodist Ladies' College at Hawthorn, a leading private school for girls. Before starting at MLC, however, Caldwell met Winifred Moverly Brown. Mrs Moverly Brown, who was childless, taught elocution.

After one year of tutoring Caldwell, who started with her at age seven, Winifred Moverly Brown became so impressed with her that she gave the little girl a very unique scholarship. She undertook to take Caldwell under her wing without charge until she was eighteen. Apart from breath control and voice development, she encouraged her to read a great deal.

"I was part of the Elocutionary Eisteddfods in Ballarat and Bendigo and won all the prizes. I was OK and bright in that department. I always stayed very much undercover because I knew my real growing up would not be in the normal Australian suburban scene. The idea of a box of Black Magic chocolates and a bunch of frangipanni being some sort of legitimate introduction to my vagina didn't seem to me to be adequate ... I find Australian men, for the most part, wildly unattractive. I find them boorish."

Caldwell's years at MLC were a sort of double life. By day, she donned the obligatory grey uniform and went through a facade of classroom activities. At night, like some character from *Cabaret*, she applied stage make-up, rinsed her hair with *red* dye and climbed into a lamé dress to work as an entertainer. Her performances consisted of recitations and songs put together for her by her mentor, Winifred Moverly Brown. She worked only at mixed functions, wedding anniversaries, twenty-first birthday celebrations — occasions of that type.

Caldwell met her first lover at a dance at the Canterbury RSL Club one Saturday evening. From fourteen to sixteen, she had a steady relationship with this boy, whom she remembers with great affection.

"I couldn't have wished for anyone better to initiate me into sex. So, quite early, actually at fourteen, I was making reasonably consistent love. Not awful, tearing, ugly love, not fucking in the back seat — but really kind of nice."

While attending MLC, Caldwell was also appearing in a radio serial produced by Morris West, based on the *Inspector Boney* novels. This had its genesis in her appearance years before in *Peter Pan* at the Tivoli when aged nine. She had played the character Slightly Soiled in this rather "raunchy" production of *Peter Pan*, starring George Formby. *Peter Pan* had been followed by a couple of years of a radio programme of 3DB where Caldwell, the intrepid child reporter, interviewed visiting celebrities.

At age twelve, when she donned the grey MLC habit, she was already much more mature than her classmates of the same age. How many MLC girls had even been to the Tivoli, let alone played the part of Slightly Soiled for the general public? This, remember, was in the days when Australian schoolgirls still had to study bowdlerised versions of *Romeo and Juliet*.

When she turned sixteen, Caldwell persuaded her parents there was little point in staying in further education. After leaving school, she spent the first year teaching elocution at a number of private schools, while continuing with her cabaret act at night. She was still undergoing instruction from Winifred Moverly Brown. She was also cast in a number of plays at the Melbourne Little Theatre, with Brett Randall, Irene Worth and George Fairfax.

When Caldwell was seventeen, she met John Sumner. Sumner had come to Melbourne from England to start the Union Theatre Repertory Company. He had seen Caldwell in a couple of the Little Theatre productions and asked her to join the rep company as resident ingenue. There was, however, a snag. Sumner had not yet arranged proper funding. Plans to engage a fulltime company had to be postponed for nine months. Caldwell took a variety of jobs. She worked for a time in a pickle factory, and as an usherette at the Regent Theatre.

Eventually, Sumner got sufficient money together and the Melbourne Rep was formed. The first company included, apart from Caldwell, two other actors who were to become well known later in other fields; Ray Lawler and Barry Humphries. Caldwell did two seasons with the Melbourne Rep. Each consisted of nine months in Melbourne wound up by a three-month tour of Victorian country towns.

While the new Melbourne Rep was evolving under the careful eye of John Sumner, up in Sydney the sagacious Dr "Nugget" Coombs of the Reserve Bank was dipping his bureaucratic fingers into a new gooey mess called the Australian Elizabethan Theatre Trust. Assisted by a couple of English types, Elsie Beyer and Hugh Hunt, Coombs was anxious to put a national theatre company together, under the Trust umbrella.

One vehicle chosen to implement this policy was Robinson Jeffers's *Medea*, written at the request of Dame Judith Anderson. Here was a classic Greek drama adapted by an American writer for an Australian actor. Hugh Hunt, chosen to direct the Australian performance, had, at that time, failed to make any impression on the English theatre. Hunt, in kneejerk English fashion, assumed Gilbert Murray to be the only worthwhile authority on Greek tragedy, and he regarded Judith Anderson as a barbarous colonial. Furthermore, arriviste Americans like Jeffers had no business fiddling round in classical Greece which only the English really understood.

The Trust's *Medea* included in its company the original actress for whom it was written, and who had played it successfully on Broadway. Despite this, Hunt managed to pluck artistic disaster from the jaws of success.

Notwithstanding the unpleasantness backstage, Caldwell was thrilled to work in *Medea*, as it involved moving from Melbourne to Sydney. She had heard much about Sydney and its wicked ways. Never having seen any other *Medea*, Australians flocked to Hugh Hunt's version, which toured the major Australian cities. Work in other Trust productions followed. Between Trust productions, Caldwell continued to play parts for the Melbourne Repertory.

In Sydney, Caldwell had moved in with an English actor who had come to Australia to play in *Medea*. She had gradually become a most important member of the Trust company. Elsie Beyer had replaced Winifred Moverly Brown as her mentor.

Beyer, the General Manager of the Trust under the mandarinate of "Nugget" Coombs, consoled Caldwell when she was not sent to London to play Buba in Ray Lawler's *Summer of the Seventeenth Doll*. Caldwell had played that role before the play went to England. Beyer

Visiting Australia, late 1960s (News Ltd)

whispered that there were other schemes afoot that would get her to London.

She warned Caldwell that if she went to London with Lawler's *Doll:* "You will always be thought of as an Australian. I have more important plans for you." The following year the Trust arranged for her to set sail (in an eight-berth cabin in the bottom of the *Oronsay*) for Britain. In her luggage was a contract with what was then called Stratford, and is now known as the Royal Shakespeare Company.

Stratford paid her £12 a week as a walk-on. Her "colonial" experience was ignored. She started again at the bottom and worked her way up. In Australia, she had been playing roles like Ophelia in *Hamlet* and Maria in *Twelfth Night*. At Stratford, she appeared as a walk-on in the chorus of *Romeo and Juliet*. Caldwell did not mind.

"Elsie Beyer was very bright. I was able to watch and observe and learn. Meanwhile, having already had much bigger responsibilities, I walked on better than anyone else. I knew how to wear clothes. I knew what to do about make-up. The following year, they sent me to Russia with the company, which was unheard of for somebody just doing walk-ons."

Within a month of her return from Russia, Caldwell had been promoted. She played Bianca in *Othello* with Paul Robson, Sam Wanamaker and Albert Finney, in the production directed by Tony Richardson.

Caldwell's Bianca caused a stir. The following season, she played it again and was also Helena in *All's Well that Ends Well*, a production directed by Tony Gutherie and starring Dame Edith Evans. She also played Cordelia in Charles Laughton's *King Lear*. All this happened in 1959, a good season for Caldwell after such a short period in England. She was becoming firmly established as a player of the first rank.

During the 1959 season, Caldwell had started an affair with Albert Finney. It became more intense and Caldwell decided her role in life was not to act but to look after Albert Finney. There was to be no 1960 season for her.

"I really always looked for the thing that Mum and Dad had, which was a real kind of mateship. I thought that's what I would have with Albert. So I came down to London (from Stratford) and I was with him when he was doing *Saturday Night and Sunday Morning* and *Billy Liar* . . . After a while, I realised that I was beginning to lose my identity. I'm squeezing the orange juice, making house, buying the sheets, keeping the house clean . . . I had been a kind of a star at Stratford, a sort of phenomenon. The thing that Mum seemed to have, which seemed to me to be so rare, was that she was very much

With husband Robert Whitehead, 1970

Dad's woman, but she was also herself. She didn't play a game with Dad. That's what I looked for ... but it's not easy to come by."

The relationship with Finney ended after two years — two years in which she had abandoned all work. She was offered a sort of escape hatch in the form of a twelve-month contract at Stratford, Ontario, in Canada. Caldwell grabbed it without asking even how much money she was to be paid. She wanted to get out of London and the memories associated with the hiatus in her life known as Albert Finney.

Caldwell spent 1961 at Stratford, Ontario. Apart from work at Stratford, there was also a lot of television work in Toronto and Winnipeg. Her strength and confidence in herself began to return. The following year, she was asked by the Australian Elizabethan Theatre Trust to return to Australia to play in their production of *Saint Joan*, which was being produced to coincide with the 1962 Adelaide Arts Festival.

Caldwell found little had changed in seven years, and she returned to something much like the fiasco produced for Dame Judith Anderson's return in 1955. Expecting to appear in an Australian production of *Saint Joan*, she found an American director, a crew of cast-off English actors, and a couple of Australians added as an afterthought. The Joan she did in Australia was not one of her best.

She did end up doing some work she enjoyed in Australia. It arose out of a meeting with Patrick White at the Adelaide Festival. They got on well and Caldwell went into two of his plays, *The Ham Funeral* followed by *The Season at Sarsaparilla*.

While doing the White plays, Caldwell became heavily involved with another man — he was a guitar-maker and a staunch Marxist filling in as a stagehand. As soon as she had finished her theatrical season, Caldwell and her guitar-maker loaded cooking pots, fishing lines and camping gear into an old Riley and headed for north Queensland. They got as far as Moreton Bay and pitched their tent. They planned to support themselves by making guitars and composing folk music. Caldwell remembers endless stews. However, Cyclone Annie arrived and, failing to recognise ideological purity, flattened their camp. They were forced to move in with a "darling" bunch of communists in a nearby commune. The delights of life in this workers' paradise did not last.

"Here I am and the men were just playing folk songs and throwing darts at John Kennedy because of the Bay of Pigs, and I was just doing the cooking like all the other women were doing the cooking. We were getting barbecues ready and all that stuff."

After a couple of months, Caldwell quietly said goodbye to her lover and slipped away from the enclave. She had an appointment in Minneapolis, Minnesota, where Tony Gutherie was establishing a new theatre company. He wanted her aboard. It would be the first time she would work in the United States, the country that was to become her home and, also, the home of the family she had been searching for.

Caldwell stayed in Minneapolis for a year, the first year of the Gutherie Theatre. She was asked to stay for a second year, but refused. By now she did not like committing herself to spending a second year in the same spot.

It is a waste of time asking Caldwell about the years between her return from Australia and her meeting with Robert Whitehead in 1966. It is not that she does not remember or that nothing important happened, but she does not deal with these memories chronologically, reflecting perhaps the whirlwind nature of her life then. She was constantly on the move from job to job, establishing an excellent reputation. There were interludes she still seems to regret. One involved an "appalling" tour of Canada in which she nonetheless made a lot of money. She promptly checked into New York's Plaza Hotel with a lover and stayed there until she blew the money.

There were great moments too. She remembers especially a television special in Toronto when she played Lady Macbeth to Sean Connery's Macbeth. Her agent then tried to talk her into going to Hollywood for a sit-com, "which I thought was just the pits and so said no". These were her "years of freedom", she was a gypsy with no fixed abode and too many suitcases. She brought her parents to North America and they all took a trip through the Rockies.

She turned thirty and suddenly noticed that interviewers were starting to ask her why she had never married. She tried to adopt a child in Minneapolis but was rejected as an unsuitable parent. On one occasion, she very nearly married: "a perfectly darling, sweet, beautiful, sexy young man. But I got as far as the preacher and realised it would have been a disaster."

Caldwell started living with the Broadway producer Robert Whitehead in 1966. A widower, he had been happily married for nineteen years before his wife died of cancer. He had met Caldwell at Stratford, Ontario, in 1965, and in New York they kept getting paired up at dinner parties. Within a few months, they were living together. The relationship remains today a remarkably strong and enduring one. The Whiteheads place family before career, and Caldwell has withdrawn from the theatre for long periods of time to attend to her family.

Professionally, Caldwell had built an impressive reputation as an actress by the time she and Whitehead started sharing the heating bill. She had made her Broadway debut in *The Devils*, filling in for Anne Bancroft while Bancroft honeymooned with Mel Brooks. Caldwell played the part on her terms and word had got around how different it was. She had then been cast as the southern gossip columnist in Tennessee Williams's *Slapstick Tragedy* which had lasted only two nights but brought Caldwell her first Tony award. There had been many other parts in both Canada and America.

In 1967, Whitehead decided to do a production of *The Prime of Miss Jean Brodie* and badly wanted Margaret Leighton for the part. He and Caldwell travelled to California to try to persuade her to do it, but Leighton was enjoying a rare patch of connubial bliss with her husband, Michael Wilding, and refused. Somebody suggested Caldwell should do the part and Whitehead and Caldwell both hooted their disapproval. However, in showbusiness nothing is ever final. Caldwell did end up doing the part and picked up a second Tony award for it into the bargain. The first award, in 1966, had been for best supporting actress. The 1968 award was the big one, for best Broadway actress of the year.

This was also the year the Whiteheads made it legal. Robert Whitehead had indicated a certain reluctance to church his lady. He indicated that he saw no merit in marriage unless Caldwell was pregnant. However, Caldwell issued an ultimatum: "We get married or I move on."

"I remember funny old Mum saying to me when I asked her why I'd never been pregnant, 'Zoe, it's just that you have never had the right nest, and when you have a nest made then something will happen'."

A date was set and Whitehead and Caldwell married in a small Bucks County church with the postmistress as matron of honour and the postman as best man. Within two months, Caldwell was pregnant. The baby was a boy — Sam — who is now in high school. Three years after him, Charlie was born. Caldwell devoted much of the 1970s to mothering her children. Since her marriage, her work as an actor has clearly been subordinated to her role as mother and wife. Given thses self-imposed limitations and the bitterly competitive nature of the profession, her achievements are the more remarkable.

In 1970, she stormed London's West End playing the fiery Emma Hamilton in a play written for her by Terence Rattigan, called *A Bequest to the Nation*. Wrote John Barber of the London *Daily Telegraph*: "This bravura Emma [is] a vulgar and foul-mouthed slut who sprawls in bed bibbing brandy before 'Me and me Nelson' become one flesh ... Miss Caldwell's tart-with-a-heart-of-gold is ribald, funny, touching, ruthless and tender, all at once."

In 1970, Caldwell also created one of her most-talked-about roles, her off-Broadway *Colette*, directed by Gerald Friedman. Over the years, there has been much talk about a Broadway *Colette* but this has not so far eventuated.

There were several other notable stage performances in the 1970s, among them *Dance of Death* (co-starring Robert Shaw) at the Lincoln Center and *Long Day's Journey into Night*, in which she played against Jason Robards Jr, at the Brooklyn Academy in 1974. The 1970s were also memorable for two superb television performances. Caldwell's *Sarah*, made for the Canadian Broadcasting Corporation, has become a television classic. For the British Broadcasting Corporation she played the role of Madame Arkadina in *The Seagull*.

In 1977, she started directing. Her first directorial task was a play called *An Almost Perfect Person*, in which her leads were Coleen Dewhurst and George Hearn. She has directed two Shakespeare productions, *Richard II* and *Othello* (both at Stratford, Ontario), and an off-Broadway play called *These Men*.

In May 1982, Caldwell took over the title role in *Medea* from Dame Judith Anderson, to whom the play is dedicated. The role had been felt to be Dame Judith's personal property for many years and Caldwell took some urging from Dame Judith to do the part. Her portrayal of Medea upset a few of the critics, who thought she was a little too lusty, but despite the criticism, she was awarded her third Tony award for the role.

Caldwell closed a circle when her production of *Medea* played Australia in the autumn and winter of 1984. Her first appearance in the play had been in 1955 as a minor player in that awful original production of *Medea*.

Caldwell, who has always refused to become an American citizen, was awarded an OBE in 1970, which seems paltry when her considerable contribution to the English-language theatre over so many years is examined. How many other Australian actresses have won three Tony awards? How many have won one?

SUMNER LOCKE ELLIOTT

Sumner Locke Elliott is a distinguished citizen of New York, where he has lived since 1948. He became an American citizen in 1955. People often think of him as being more strongly Australian than he really is. This is especially true after seeing Jill Robb's film *Careful He Might Hear You*, based on the autobiographical novel by Elliott.

The circumstances of Sumner Locke Elliott's birth have dominated his life and work. His mother died when he was born in 1917, leaving her son her name, Sumner Locke. What Elliott knows about his mother, who was also a writer, he learnt from another Australian author Katharine Susannah Prichard.

Elliott's father, Henry Logan Elliott, was a paymaster in the First AIF. Logan Elliott died in 1939, but his son saw him only once, on a railway station getting on the Melbourne Express in uniform. Elliott was three at the time, yet the memory is still vivid. There was one other communication. On his twenty-first birthday, a telegram from Logan Elliott arrived: "Congratulations on reaching your majority." When Elliott's mother died, her two sisters took over his care. As he grew older, his father's absence pressed heavily upon him. Absence can often be more inexplicable and worrying to a child than death.

Elliott's two aunts lived on different sides of Sydney; Aunt Lily, who voted Labor, at Banksia and Aunt Jessie, who did not vote Labor, at Point Piper. When Elliott was ten, the two sisters took their squabble over custody of their nephew to the Supreme Court. Elliott (who wanted to live with Lily) based the courtroom scenes in *Careful He Might Hear You* on records of his own case. After Elliott talked to the Judge in Chambers (he was too young to give evidence on oath), a compromise was reached. He was to spend alternate weekends at Banksia and Point Piper and attend Cranbrook School in Sydney's Eastern Suburbs as a boarder, at Lily's expense.

Elliott is not an enthusiastic Old Cranbrookian. He loathed everything about the school, where he spent two years as a boarder, and a third year as a day-boy after contracting scarlet fever. At the beginning of 1929, rich Aunt Jessie died. (In the book, and later the movie, the time-frame of these events has been changed to include the Depression.) Jessie's death finally severed his connection with Cranbrook and left him in the sole charge of his Aunt Lily. He spent the next three years at Neutral Bay High School and, after repeating

---

Sumner Locke Elliott, Sydney, 1980 (News Ltd)

the second year, obtained his Intermediate Certificate in 1933, aged sixteen.

On the general question of scholarship, Elliott is mildly skeptical:

"Brilliant scholars, especially if they are good in everything, become jack-of-all-trades and they do not sustain themselves in any particular branch of learning. I finished about thirty-sixth from the top in a class of forty ... The boy most likely to succeed at school is the boy you never hear of again."

In 1934, the Great Depression raged in Sydney. Elliott enrolled in French courses at the Berlitz and in classes in typing and journalism. The classes were paid for by "one of my numerous other aunts who wished to contribute to my education". He took a twelve-week course in syntax and grammar, "which have never been very good. My spelling in those days was appalling."

Before Elliott was ten, he had written his first play, for a toy theatre he had been given for Christmas. At Neutral Bay High School he wrote a play for Speech Day called *The Twins of Twinmount* in which he allotted the starring role to himself. The following year, he returned to the boards in another melodrama set on the Cornish cliffs in which he played an eighty-five-year-old fisherman. At the age of fifteen, Elliott launched a full-frontal attack on the formidable figure of Doris Fitton at the Independent Theatre. He marched in to see her with twenty-seven one-act plays under his arm.

If there is a renaissance in Australian theatre today, Doris Fitton kept the flame flickering through the long night of the Dark Ages. In the 1930s, she was the only hope in Sydney for tyros like Elliott. One of his "awful one-acters" was given a studio reading at the Independent and in due course he made his acting debut there, as an office boy in the Independent's production of *The Fugitive* by John Galsworthy. A few years later, in 1938, his first three-act play, *The Cow Jumped Over the Moon*, was performed there.

"There were always two sides to me. One was the actor and the other was the writer. I never wanted to be a writer. It may have been because my mother's books were always around and I never liked many of her friends. They were peculiar to me.

"I liked writing one-act plays, because I could always include a part for me. I had a dual life for most of my career in Australia, which lasted from 1934 until I left for America in 1948.

"I've always said the greatest experience in playwriting is to act in other people's plays. I think a good playwright, even if he only comes on as the handyman or the butler, gets in this way to better understand the mechanics of writing.

"It was like getting an OBE when I wrote my first three-act play. It was a silly little comedy, fearfully derivative of early Fredrick Londsdale. At the end [it ran for three nights at Doris Fitton's Independent Club rooms] Doris patted my knee and said, 'You're a very clever young boy'."

Work for the Independent was unpaid. There was no government support for the arts in the 1930s. Any job was hard to get but particularly one in the theatre. Elliott was fortunate to pick up a position in the publicity office of J. C. Williamson's, but for a time was unable to work directly for the stage, either acting or writing. Then, in 1937, not yet twenty-one, Elliott joined George Edwards and Nell Sterling, who produced radio serials, as a £5-a-week scriptwriter. George Edwards was known as "The Man with a Thousand Voices".

Elliott's first task was to write fifty-two episodes of a children's serial called "David and Dawn and the Sea Fairies". He had to churn out five or six episodes of this serial each day, dictating the breathless dialogue to a typist. Each episode ran between twelve and twelve and a half minutes — six and a half pages of double-spaced dialogue. If an episode went well, he could dictate it in forty minutes, but even if there were difficulties he could not afford to spend much more than an hour on any one episode, or he would drop too far behind. Often he did not know what the next page would contain.

"You had to have a cliff-hanger ending each night, four nights a week. They were terrible things. [It was] just trash I wrote in those days; but it served its purpose."

Elliott's duties, as well as writing, included answering the telephones, directing the work of the typing pool and performing whatever parts were allotted to him in Edwards-Sterling productions.

His evenings and weekends were spent at the Independent Theatre and its club rooms. Miss Fitton was now Doris. His list of Independent acting credits range from roles in *Hamlet* to *The Little Foxes*. His writing credits for George Edwards Productions include such Gothic heart-stoppers as fifty-two episodes of "Hard Cash", "Jezabel's Daughter" and "Scarlet Rhapsody".

Elliott continued to live with Aunt Lily. Her husband, George, had died in 1930, and she and Elliott had moved to Cremorne. Except for his service in the army, Elliott was to remain under Lily's roof until he left Australia in 1948.

When the Second World War started in 1939, Elliott was given his ninety-day basic training and allowed to return to civilian life. His employer, George Edwards, managed to prevent his call-up until the end of 1941. Edwards argued with the authorities that the radio programmes Elliott was writing were crucial to morale for civilians and the armed forces. Following the Japanese attack on Pearl Harbor and the collapse of the Allied army in Malaya, however, Elliott was called up for service in January 1942. He remained a member of the Australian Military Forces until April 1946.

The war years saw several of his plays performed at the Independent Theatre. For some time, Elliott was stationed in Sydney and continued to perform in Independent productions. His play *Interval* was produced in 1939 and published in 1941. In 1940, *The Little Sheep Run Fast* and in 1942, *Goodbye to the Music* were performed. In 1943, it was *Your Obedient Servant. Invisible Circus* was performed just after the war, in 1946, while Elliott was still in uniform. Of his army service, Elliott recalls:

"I typed my way through the war. I was a class-A army typist ... It did preclude me from going into the infantry and having to go to New Guinea. I was always safe and dry."

Elliott wrote *Rusty Bugles* after the war ended, while awaiting discharge. He wrote it about Mataranka Ordinance Depot in the Northern Territory where he had been stationed in 1944, partly to lay those years to rest and partly because he found himself sitting in an army depot in Sydney with nothing to do. Once written, *Bugles* was to remain unperformed for three years.

Rusty Bugles is not the only Elliott work to draw on his army years. Readers of *Water Under the Bridge*, published in 1978, will recall in particular the two girls who work in the camouflage netting department. For several months in 1942, Elliott was stationed at Sydney's Victoria Barracks, in the section handling camouflage netting. To this day, he speaks bitterly of this experience. He cannot forget the smell associated with the netting which was almost impossible to remove. He was convinced people edged away from him in the bus on his way home from Victoria Barracks each evening.

Elliott's first postwar problem was to get out of the army. According to the point system which governed the order of discharge, he would be lucky to be released by the end of 1946. He had spent the last part of the war as a writer with the rank of staff sergeant on "The Army Hour", which was broadcast with considerable distaste by the ABC and dumped as soon as the Japanese surrendered. Now his commanding officer in the entertainment unit, Jim

---

With Gordon Chater (right) in a Minerva Theatre Production, Sydney, late 1940s

Davidson, offered to expedite his discharge if he signed a contract with David N. Martin and the Tivoli circuit to appear in a new Tivoli show in Melbourne. Jim Davidson was producing the show. Staff Sergeant Elliott agreed — "I had nothing else to do" — and four days later he was a civilian. Elliott hated his three months at the Melbourne Tivoli. Jim Davidson himself quit on opening night. After three months, the show moved to Sydney. Elliott was home again, but this time for the last time.

Elliott had been listed at the American Consulate as a potential migrant since 1938. A friend who had married an American during the war arranged for her husband to sponsor him as a migrant. His immigration papers finally came through in 1948, and he left in July of that year. Of his decision to emigrate, Elliott says:

"I am firmly convinced that I was attracted to America in my mother's womb. She was attracted to America and Americans, unlike the drift going the other way to the 'old' country. I was always very defensive with English people. They would come and patronise the hell out of you in Australia. Americans have other faults but they never patronise. I don't know what would have happened if I'd gone and settled in London. I might have become a second-rate playwright in the West End, and written what would be now very dated Terence Rattigan-type plays."

During his last two years in Sydney, Elliott worked regularly for his old employer, George Edwards Productions. He performed often on the "Lux Radio Theatre", and wrote for "Lux" its first original script, "Wicked is the Vine".

At the Independent Theatre in North Sydney, Doris Fitton was frightened to touch *Rusty Bugles*. She felt the public was sick of the war and wartime humour. As the time of Elliott's departure approached, however, the Independent Theatre decided to give him a farewell supper followed by a reading of one of his plays. Elliott persuaded them to read the still-unperformed *Bugles*. A few old uniforms were dug up and a cast assembled to read the parts in a couple of mock sets. The reading was an unexpected sensation; the tiny theatre had rarely heard such laughter. Instant plans were made for the production of *Rusty Bugles* and it opened two months after Elliott left Australia. When he returned to Australia almost two years later, *Bugles* had just closed. He has still to see this play performed.

Bugles attracted the attention of the New South Wales Vice Squad and the Chief Secretary when it opened in Sydney. Questions were asked in Parliament and there was an uproar about the rawness of its language. Doris Fitton had to haggle over individual words in the script with the Vice Squad to keep the biggest hit the Independent had ever had running. As is usual, the attentions of the custodians of public morality created considerable interest in the play, and substantially increased its run.

While *Rusty Bugles* were blowing in Sydney, cold winds were blowing in New York. *Bugles*'s success in Sydney could not even help Elliott financially. He was not permitted by the Australian authorities to transfer his royalties to America.

After leaving Sydney in July, Elliott had paused in Los Angeles on his way to New York. Ron Randall, the Australian actor, and other Australian members of the Hollywood film colony entertained him. It was a pleasant interlude with visits, in long, sleek cars, to film studios, and the pool at the Beverly Hills Hotel. His first impression of Hollywood was favourable. Later, he would grow to despise California and, most of all, Los Angeles.

His first months in New York were uncomfortable. He stayed with old friends, the parents of two noisy children, in the New York suburb of Queens. Elliott was, for the first three months, homesick.

"I arrived in summer. New York summer is a vendetta against human nature unless you have air-conditioning. It's also a bad time to get around to see people. I had dozens of letters of introduction. I took my radio scripts around and my publicity. People were extraordinarily kind to me, but I needed money, and I needed it badly. I was earning a lot of money from *Rusty Bugles* but I couldn't get it out of the country. I had to move to a rather dirty little room on East 31st Street."

One important step remained in his transformation. In Australia, Elliott had been both an actor and a writer. He soon realised it would be impossible to maintain both careers in New York, and chose writing.

Elliott's cash eroded steadily and he started to get worried. He accepted an invitation one night to a party, more for the free drinks and hors d'oeuvres than for the entertainment. He arrived feeling particularly shabby.

"I got into conversation with this woman who was in her forties, and she said to me, 'What do you do?' and I said, 'I write', and she said, 'What are you writing?' and I said, 'I'm not writing anything. I'm caught in this terrible jam. I have no money and I really have got to write to earn some. I've got to write, desperately, but I'm so uptight with the fact that I have no money that I can't write, so it's a vicious circle.'

"It turned out she was a nurse from Bellevue Hospital and she said, 'Isn't that strange? Our next-door neighbour is the top story editor at CBS, if that would be any help to you.'

"A week later I was walking up Fifth Avenue and I suddenly thought I had better call this man because she may have got in touch with him. To my utter surprise he said: 'Where are you this very minute? Come around.'"

Elliott met Arthur Heinman that afternoon. They talked about his background in Australian theatre and radio. When TV started, it was run by executives who had cut their teeth on radio rather than the movies. A few weeks after Elliott's meeting with Heinman, he got an urgent call from CBS to meet with Worthington Miner, producer of Westinghouse's "Studio One", a dramatic anthology programme televised live from New York on Monday nights.

Miner's problem was fairly straightforward. W. Somerset Maugham's novel *Of Human Bondage* was due to be televised in ten days and the radio writer he had engaged to produce a television script had turned in an unusable one. He had spent most of his budget on the rejected script. Could Elliott do a television version of *Of Human Bondage* by Friday for $200. Elliott's heart soared and he announced that for $200, "I can also do *War and Peace*".

He was told to forget the first 200 pages of Maugham's story and start at the point where Philip the young medico meets Mildred the Cockney waitress. He was to reduce the novel to a one-hour script, allowing time for commercials, and preserving all major ingredients of the story. Ten days later, Sumner Locke Elliott's heavily reduced version of *Of Human Bondage* went to air, starring Charlton Heston (at that time unknown) and Felicia Montealegre (now Mrs Leonard Bernstein).

This was to be the start of a seven-year stint as a writer during the golden years of television drama. Unfortunately, very few of these early television plays survive in broadcastable quality. They were performed live in New York and recorded by an inefficient cinefilm technique known as kinescoping.

Following his successful Maugham adaptation, Elliott was given *Jane Eyre* to adapt. Gradually he worked his way through the English classics. The producers had convinced themselves that Elliott was a master of English idioms and accents, particularly Cockney, which American writers had terrible trouble with.

"I could do a fake Cockney which might not have gone over very

Author of *Careful He Might Hear You*, early 1960s (News Ltd)

well at the BBC, but it was perfectly acceptable in America."

After he had been in New York for eighteen months, Elliott was forced to return quickly to Sydney by the news that Aunt Lily was dying. It was a trip he hated making. He was concerned about the interruption to his burgeoning career and, more importantly, about being allowed back into America. Between the time his plane took off from Honolulu and the time it landed in Sydney, the Korean War had started. This intensified Elliott's fears, and his nerves finally produced a severe attack of shingles. When he returned to New York after two months, he suffered recurring nightmares about the trip.

"I used to dream that I'd get on a Madison Avenue bus and I'd step off in Hunter Street, or Martin Place. It was a classic nightmare. I'd get on a train to, say, go to Chicago and I'd arrive in Hornsby or Katoomba."

This occasioned a "sort of phobia" about Australia that took many years to dissolve. Elliott did not return for twenty-four years, not until he went back as the guest of honour for Writers' Week at the 1974 Adelaide Festival.

Before he had left for Australia on that first trip back, Elliott had decided to move from "Studio One" to the "Philco Theatre". He now made one of the biggest connections of his career when he met there the producer Fred Coe. "Philco Theatre" produced only original works, a welcome change after adapting classics. Each writer wrote seven or eight teleplays a year, and the stable included such names as Paddy Chayefsky, Horton Foote, Tad Mosel and Robert Arthur Allen. Gore Vidal worked there briefly.

Three directors were associated with "Philco Theatre", Arthur Penn (later of *Bonnie and Clyde* fame), Delbert Mann and Vincent Donahue. The writers worked closely with both the directors and the actors, a great many of whom were "method" actors who often came directly from classes at the Lee Strasberg Acting School. Elliott recalls regular appearances by Kim Stanley, Eve Marie Saint, Rod Steiger, Jo Van Fleet and E. G. Marshall. The close association with Fred Coe continued during the early and middle 1950s, Eliott writing nineteen plays for him.

"It lasted until the coming of tape, the coming of colour and the coming of what we now know as the special. These developments veered away from original writing into the old and well-known properties. Genuinely original writing is now practically gone from television."

As the demand for original television drama faded, Elliott became involved once more in adaptations. It was the beginning of television's continuing love affair with big-budget specials. He wrote several of these. One of them, "The King and Mrs Candle", which starred Australian Cyril Ritchard and Joan Greenwood, was an original musical. The rest were adaptations. As the budgets sky-rocketed:

"... It all began to get very much more involved with the big Hollywood star names; it became very much less interesting to the writer. The stars got bigger and the writer got smaller. I knew that sooner or later it was all going to leave New York. I despise California, especially Los Angeles. It's just the dreariness of it all, the pinkness of it all. It's Death Valley! It was a terrible time because all my friends were leaving, one by one, and moving there."

Searching round for something to replace television drama, Elliott did a documentary with Hedda Hopper about the legendary Hollywood stars of past and present. When it was over, he decided to turn it into a magazine article. It was the first time he had ever written prose. The piece was published by America's oldest magazine, *Harper's*.

"I began to find that this was very interesting, that I could explore and go into people's minds, and that it was a solo effort. For the first time in my life, it was just me."

This was the genesis of Elliott's first novel, *Careful He Might Hear You*, which he had first thought of as a play but abandoned because of its complexity, its large number of characters and locations. The novel took two years to write, during which Elliott did two final sad television shows for Fred Coe, completing his last work in that medium on two Hitchcock adaptations.

Harper and Row bought the novel. So did the Reader's Digest Book Club, and it was translated into several languages. *Careful He Might Hear You* was published in 1963. Elliott in his mid-forties, having long resisted the novel form "because of the shadow of my mother", was now a successful author. He describes *Careful He Might Hear You* as a clearing-out, a "ghost-catching".

"I didn't find it painful to write. I found myself very removed from those times. I didn't ever — and I think it was wise — think of myself as the little boy. It cleared the way, however, for me to go on to other things."

Elliott's second novel, *Doves and Pythons*, was published three years later in 1966 and was based on the life of a friend who was a theatrical agent. Elliott recently observed that the subject of the book has never really forgiven him for it. Much of the book is set in a little village in Bucks County frequented by actors, directors and writers.

Doves and Pythons was not as well received as *Careful He Might Hear You*, the frequent fate of second novels.

Eden's Lost, published three years after his second book, in 1969, opens in Australia's Blue Mountains, moves to wartime Sydney and finishes in New York's Long Island, each segment seen from the point of view of a different character. The assortment of characters who parade through its pages are witty, eccentric and often degenerate. Yet it is not a cruel book. There is compassion for those who have fallen by the wayside and a shrewd and witty commentary on those who have passed them by.

Working like a metronome to his three-year schedule, Elliott's next book, *The Man Who Got Away*, was published in 1972. In this one, Elliott produces yet another structure, this time of a sci-fi sort. In *The Man Who Got Away*, a forty-three-year-old man slips backwards in time. The reader observes the crucial moments in the protagonist's life reeling backwards. This allows Elliott to reveal his hero with all his neurotic tendencies fully developed in middle life and then, by unwinding the clock, he shows how these traits developed.

Going (1974) was Elliott's most controversial book. This futuristic story posited an American society ruled by emotionless functionaries who claim to "love" everybody but are incapable of any feeling. One rule of this new order is that all citizens are put down like faithful dogs on their sixty-fifth birthday. Elliott's heroine, Tess Bracken, is a selfish old bitch who is due to be called for and put down, as it is her sixty-fifth birthday. On this last day of her life, Tess gets in touch with her feelings for other people and finally, after escaping to Canada, returns by choice to face her own liquidation. To describe *Going* as a flop is a little strong, but of all Elliott's novels, it comes nearest to answering that description.

In *Water Under the Bridge* (1977), Elliott returns to his native setting in Australia. This may be merely a matter of convenience for an author who has said he writes in time rather than space. *Water Under the Bridge*, like all Elliott's novels, seems to have as its underlying mood the themes of despair and solitude. There is a line in *Water Under the Bridge* that has been widely quoted in reviews. Maggie McGhee says, "Everybody's a failure at four o'clock in the morning in the dark".

In *Signs of Life* (1982), he returns to America. It's about a woman, aged eighty-one, who is dying, and finally reaches some accommoda-

---

Publicising *Signs of Life*, United States, 1981

tion with herself and her past through the daughter with whom she has fought bitterly.

Elliott lives, as he has done for almost twenty years, in a modest but pleasant apartment on a quiet street on the east side of Manhattan. At a small period desk in the sitting-room, near the window, sits a very old portable typewriter. Now in his middle sixties, Elliott finds he can write only in the early morning. By mid-morning, his mood changes and he carefully locks his work away and the rest of his day begins.

This is much what you would expect for a single man of his age and interests in Manhattan. There are not many plays for him any more. He is getting picky about what he will sit through for three hours. Every summer, he goes to New Hampshire to escape the oppressive heat. He loves New York the rest of the year.

Elliott has long since got over his phobia about visiting Australia. He did not make another visit until 1974 when he was asked to Writers' Week at the Adelaide Festival, and he has since returned in 1978 and 1980. He is happy at the revival of interest in his work in Australia, which started when *Water Under the Bridge* was made into a television series. The movie version of *Careful He Might Hear You* won many Australian movie awards in 1983. After thirty-six years, Elliott has been absorbed into the mainstream of Manhattan. This is the town that gave him his career — first as a television writer and then as a novelist — and in which he has worked so long. And yet the underlying theme of all his novels is the lonely cry of the bewildered Australian orphan. His acute characterisation, his compassion, even his bitter wit, are the products of his eternal quest for the parents who never were. What happens late at night when he can't sleep? Then, one suspects, his mind wanders uneasily back to the land of his birth and troubled youth. At least he has the consolation that from his private bewilderment he has created a body of public work that looks more durable each year.